T0194765

WHAT NOBODY KNOWS

M. A. SLATTON

WESTBOW
PRESS®
A DIVISION OF THOMAS NELSON
& ZONDERVAN

This book is a work of non-fiction. Unless otherwise noted, the author and the publisher make no explicit guarantees as to the accuracy of the information contained in this book and in some cases, names of people and places have been altered to protect their privacy.

WestBow Press books may be ordered through booksellers or by contacting:

WestBow Press
A Division of Thomas Nelson & Zondervan
1663 Liberty Drive
Bloomington, IN 47403
www.westbowpress.com
844-714-3454

Because of the dynamic nature of the Internet, any web addresses or links contained in this book may have changed since publication and may no longer be valid. The views expressed in this work are solely those of the author and do not necessarily reflect the views of the publisher, and the publisher hereby disclaims any responsibility for them.

Any people depicted in stock imagery provided by Getty Images are models, and such images are being used for illustrative purposes only. Certain stock imagery © Getty Images.

Scripture quotations, unless otherwise stated, are from The Holy Bible, English Standard Version® (ESV®), copyright © 2001 by Crossway Bibles, a publishing ministry of Good News Publishers. Used by permission. All rights reserved.

Scripture quotations marked AMP are taken from the Amplified® Bible, Copyright © 1954, 1958, 1962, 1964, 1965, 1987 by The Lockman Foundation. Used by permission.

Scripture quotations marked KJV are taken from the Holy Bible, King James Version.

ISBN: 979-8-3850-0051-7 (sc)
ISBN: 979-8-3850-0050-0 (hc)
ISBN: 979-8-3850-0127-9 (e)

Library of Congress Control Number: 2023911409

Print information available on the last page.

WestBow Press rev. date: 06/28/2023

NOTES

Although some grammar experts may disagree, I have chosen to capitalize pronouns referring to my Lord out of reverence for His person, which should never go unrecognized for a single word.

I also refer to the third member of the Holy Trinity as simply Holy Spirit instead of *the* Holy Spirit. We don't say *the Jesus,* do we? Since I have no other proper name for Him, as I do with the Son, I call Him Holy Spirit just so we remember He's a person, not a thing.

I have not written out every scripture. I invite each reader to grab their Bible and read for themselves. Maybe it will lead to an even greater revelation. If it does, this whole book is worth it.

To Rebecca
God's somebody

CONTENTS

SECTION 4: NOBODY'S THINKING: ANSWERING THE QUESTIONS

SECTION 5: NOBODY REMEMBERS: KEEPING AN EYE ON THE GOAL

SECTION 6: NOBODY'S PRAYING: WHY SHOULD WE?

SECTION 7: NOBODY WAS THERE: THE ETERNAL NOW

INTRODUCTION

If you go into your local bookstore, you will not find my name on the cover of any other book there. I am not a well-known person. In fact, as of this moment, only a few people know my name. I am like all the rest of the "faceless masses." I do what I can to make the best of what I have. As a Christian, I pray that the Lord will help me not to screw up my witness and to be an effective representative for Him.

Beyond that, I could most logically say I am invisible. I am nobody. Yep. This book is about my own experiences and moments of revelation.

Pretty selfish, isn't it? But I guess I have the idea that I am not the only painfully self-conscious nobody out there. This is a compilation of lessons learned, not the story of my life. But I like to think that if a person were a good enough storyteller, they could show how interesting anyone's life really is.

Every person has their own unique experience. I am the only one living my life. You are the only one living yours. And I believe that even if our lives are not attractive to anyone else, they are most certainly interesting to God.

The truth is there are many seemingly invisible people on the earth. People seem to see us when we're standing right in front of them. They conduct business, make small talk, maybe laugh, or otherwise respond to who's in front of them. But when we step away, we're forgotten. Just that quickly, we simply go out of their head. We blend into the background, like one blade of grass or a single flower does not stand out in a field of the same or one leaf on a summer tree does not rustle in a more exciting way than the rest.

It seems like we have become no one. We see our lives passing without event or comment. We may be trampled like the grass without anyone's conscience being pricked. We may fall to the ground like autumn castoffs, but it doesn't matter. We will be replaced, and life goes on.

But people are not just grass, flowers, or leaves. Each individual has a God-given purpose. We touch one another in ways we are not aware of. We change the world by our existence and reshape the paths by our footprints.

Whatever we give will make a difference, like the proverbial ripples on a pond forever moving outward, touching other ripples, and bouncing off unmovable stone until it's worn down to dust, a smoother path one day. Whatever we move out of place becomes a stumbling block. The more people who stumble, the more hurt and anger we add to the world by the smallest acts of selfishness in a seemingly invisible life.

Invisible people make the world easier or harder, one small ripple or stone at a time. So many of them. So many invisible people not thought of, not sought, and not considered. But still important. I have to believe that. I have to, because I'm one of them. But I have a Friend who is beyond any somebody. He is *the* Somebody. So just for a moment, I will step onto this empty stage and tell you what this nobody knows, what seems true and important. I hope, with God's help, it will make a difference.

SECTION 1

NOBODY'S BEING CAREFUL:
THERE'S A REASON FOR EVERYTHING

1

THE ONE PURPOSE

I will warn you now I love words and definitions of words. So often, we don't really understand what we are communicating or what is being communicated to us. I have found that a dictionary is a wonderful thing. For instance, the word *purpose* means the intention, the goal, the plan, or the target of something. I have long since lost count of how many times I've heard the confused and exasperated statement on the lips of fellow Christians "I just don't know what my purpose is!"

Generally, the person saying this is lumping together all manner of expectations with a feeling of complete inadequacy.

We all tend to compare ourselves with others. We all wish we could do or be certain things. This often encompasses talents or accomplishments we see in others that we would love to see in ourselves, but they just aren't there. It doesn't help that people who do find some level of success add to our general feeling of failure by proclaiming, "If I can do it, anybody can!"

Like it or not, we are just not all wired or programmed the same. So we cannot find our purpose in life by observing the accomplishments of others. Not everyone is a public speaker. As an often-contented loner, I can affirm that some are not even very good private speakers. In Christian circles, not everyone is an evangelist or a teacher or equipped to sing on the worship team.

So would you think I was deluding myself if I said I believe we all have the same ultimate purpose from the most remarkable, most accomplished person to the apparently least talented or most ignored? God created us all as individuals with a single goal. It's just that His purpose is accomplished through all manner of methods by a wise heavenly Father who knows what it will take for each of us to get where He's taking us. We must guard our hearts and be careful not even to consider that we are being neglected or missing out on the blessings.

So what is God's purpose? It has nothing to do with how successful we look in this life. It has everything to do with our Lord preparing us to step into His eternal kingdom. His purpose is that each of us conform to His image, learn to hear His voice, and walk in obedience to Him. His goal is that we know Him. His goal is that we be with Him forever. Since He made each of us uniquely, it requires a unique life for each of us to realize His purpose for us.

♥

Who am I?
And who are you?
What are we here for anyway?
Is there really a reason?
The one who made us all
Knows the reason for everything.
He knows why this world,
This tiny speck in the universe,
Is our transient home.

We are the privileged ones.
We get to walk down this short hallway
We call life on earth.
Only those who do so
Can reach the end He has created for us.

We are the product of His heart,
Made to live as His children,
Made to know Him as no others do.
Everything we do, say, and believe
Brings us closer or pushes us away
From that purpose.

We are all different.
We each require different forces,
Different challenges,
To get us to where we're going.

Some need to overcome the temptations of riches.
Some need to find joy in poverty.
Some need to stand before masses without arrogance.
Some need to sit alone without feeling neglected.
Some need to serve with strength.
Some need to find joy in weakness.

We all must pass through the doors we open when He knocks—
The door of faith,
The door of love,
The door of obedience—
And we all step through the same doorway at the end of the journey.

This is our purpose:
To be prepared through whatever life holds for us,
To be prepared to take up our appointed place—
Beyond every door, beyond time, beyond ourselves.

Our purpose is one thing:
To be with Him, to take our place in His kingdom.

Are you ready yet?

What Somebody said: Psalm 57:2, 138:8; Ephesians 1:5–6, 11–12;
2 Timothy 1:9–10

2

LEGALESE: THE COVENANT

I'm sure I'm not the only one to have noticed how little trust can be placed in the words of most people. Men, women, and even children will say whatever gains them the advantage or appears to protect them in any given situation. I have observed this among politicians and churchgoers, movie stars and homeless people, toddlers and the elderly. Jesus noticed it, too, and knew better than to place His trust in people. (See John 2:24–25.) Even though He had made a covenant with them, He knew they could not be trusted to keep it.

What is a covenant anyway? It is an ancient word, and the significance and seriousness of it have become largely lost to the consciousness of modern society. Many people may immediately think of marriage as a covenant. But it's not a covenant important enough to keep a disturbing number from being permanently broken. Worldwide, the divorce rate has risen over 250 percent since 1960. And among major religions, Christians have the highest divorce rate.

Everyone believes they have a good reason for breaking that covenant, and I am certainly not the one to pass judgment. This is just one universal example of how trivial covenants have become to many people.

Again, what is a covenant? By definition, it's a formal, solemn, binding agreement. A covenant is often a written agreement or promise, signed and sealed by two or more parties for the performance of some action. The Old Testament and New Testament can also be called the old and new covenants. They are full of covenant language and intent, sealed by law and sacrifice. And we, as believers, are part of God's covenant with humankind.

The whole of the scriptures could be viewed as a legal document as well as instructions in faith. It is God's formal statement of how He will use, and limit, the activities of His limitless powers toward humankind. It is also how humankind can come into agreement with God and enjoy the benefits of relationship with Him. Finally, it details the consequences of failing to obey the clear dictates of the Maker and Owner of the earth and everything on it, including human beings. (See Deut. 30:19; John 3:18–19.)

In ancient times, covenants were often sealed with blood. One example would be in Genesis 15, when God made a covenant to bless Abraham and his descendants. Abraham slaughtered the animals God commanded and split them in half on the ground. We read that God passed between the parts of the carcasses and promised Abraham the land of Canaan for his inheritance, descendants too numerous to count, and blessings extending to every nation of the world.

Although it was customary in that part of the world for both parties to pass between the pieces during the covenant ceremony, on this occasion God caused Abraham to be incapacitated while He walked through alone. Why is this?

I can only tell you what seems right to me, and you may judge for yourself. There was an excellent reason for the way God made His covenant with Abraham and the descendants who would come after him. The one who passed between the animals pledged to keep his word. He was saying, "Let what happened to these animals happen to me if this covenant should ever be broken."

God knew that Abraham, even with his great faith, could never fulfill that covenant. God knew that Abraham's faith would quickly be lost in future generations. And God knew it would take blood to restore the broken promise of the covenant (Hebrews 9:22). God took that whole covenant upon Himself, knowing He must pay the price for its brokenness one day on a cross (Hebrews 9:11–12). He took the covenant seriously. He still does. So we can absolutely trust His ability to fulfill His part of the legal agreement between God and humankind.

♥

I believe.
Really, I do.
I believe that every word is true.
I believe that every promise is sure.
I believe that You are God.
I believe that You love me.
I believe it all.

But I am often a fool.
Yes, I admit it.
I speak foolish words.
I do foolish things.
Like Job, I speak of things I know nothing about.
I am often proved wrong.

I am selfish.
I am afraid.
I am small in my thinking.
I am small in my giving.
I am overgrown with weeds of pride and rejection,
All tangled up in my own lack.

But You are generous.
You are faithful.
You are forever offering me freedom.

You are forever loving me.
You are forever pulling me out of the mire,
Removing the guilt that clings to me
And granting me favor.

Who does such things?
Who forgives the fallen, the unfaithful?
Who sets free the condemned?
How does that happen?
I am so glad You are who You are.
I am so glad to be Your child, Your sheep,
Part of Your family.

By an eternal covenant, I have been granted access.
By an unbreakable agreement, I have been given life.
By omnipotent design I have become a royal citizen.
By Your own determination I have been chosen.
I am awestruck, speechless.
You are beyond comprehension.
And I will love You forever.

What Somebody said: Psalm 105:7–8; Jeremiah 31:33–34; Matthew 26:27–28; Hebrews 8:6, 9:18, 13:20–21

$\gg 3 \ll$

PRIDE AND HUMILITY: WHAT'S THE DIFFERENCE?

It may seem like a ridiculous question. Everyone knows the difference between pride and humility, right?

I'm not so sure about that.

Many years ago, I heard a short teaching presented by a Bible college student. I don't remember his name, but his brief lesson had a profound impact on my life that continues decades later. There was a good reason I happened to be there, that I heard that lesson. I needed it, and as I have observed people over the years, it seems others need it too. Plus it's a remarkable story, so I ask you to indulge me a bit here.

I will share the lesson as I remember it. The biblical reference on which the study is based is the first two kings of Israel, Saul and David. You can read their story beginning in the ninth chapter of 1 Samuel. Saul was quite the manly specimen, head and shoulders taller than anyone else. He was from the tribe of Benjamin, which had almost been completely wiped out during the time of the judges. Saul also described his family as the least significant in the tribe. He didn't think much of the idea of himself becoming king. After all, he was just a humble nobody.

Nevertheless, after Israel had demanded a king and at God's instructions, Samuel anointed Saul and sent him on his way. When Saul went home, he didn't initially change his daily routine for the whole king thing. Maybe he thought nothing would come of it if he just ignored it. Maybe the concept was just too terrifying to contemplate. Maybe he was still trying to hide as he had among the baggage on the day he was publicly chosen. Saul tried to carry on business as usual. He was a pretty humble guy.

Yes, so far, Saul appears to be humble. He didn't put on airs, wear a crown, build a throne, or create a royal court. He just went home. Of course, that didn't last. When Israel was attacked, everyone looked to the anointed king to act. Saul was able to rally the troops and win the victory. This made everyone happy with their new monarch, and Saul's reign became one of military might.

Now let's cut to David for a moment. David and Saul both grew up as country boys caring for their fathers' livestock. David certainly had no reason to be proud as the youngest of eight brothers—by all accounts the runt of the litter. He was relegated to tending the sheep, which meant many days of solitary existence in the wilderness. I can picture him sitting on a rocky outcropping with his harp in hand, making up tunes that calmed sheep and shepherd alike. But in his heart and mind, David knew he was more than a shepherd. He had faith and skills, and he was not afraid to use them.

While David wiled away his time with the flocks, practicing slinging stones at small predators and slaying the occasional bear or lion that threatened the herd, King Saul was experiencing the first real test of his faith and character. The Philistines had amassed an insurmountable force against the Israelite army. The prophet Samuel had instructed Saul to wait for him for seven days, but as the seventh day progressed and Samuel had yet to appear, both the troops and Saul began to panic.

The Israelite soldiers were beginning to desert their new king.

Many had fled to hide in caves, among the rocks, or even in cisterns. Saul finally gave in to the fear and anxiety. He needed God to be on his side, so he performed the sacrifice himself instead of waiting for Samuel. Of course, Samuel showed up just as he was completing those sacrifices, and it was all over for Saul.

This wasn't the only time Saul was disobedient to God, favoring public opinion and giving in to the pressure of the crowd. In 1 Samuel 15, we find him compromising again. It may appear on the surface that Saul was just too humble to lift himself as the leader and say no to the people. After all, who was he in the face of an entire nation? He was still just a lesser son of a lesser tribe, not qualified for the role God had imposed on him.

Back to David. David's father sent him to check on his older brothers, who were soldiers in Saul's army, again facing the Philistines. David arrives in time to hear giant Goliath give his arrogant challenge to Israel. Goliath dared them to send one warrior to fight him alone, winner take all.

Little David immediately wanted to know who this foul pagan thought he was. David was ready to take him on. He boldly told Saul, "The LORD who delivered me from the paw of the lion and from the paw of the bear will deliver me from the hand of this Philistine" (1 Samuel 17:37).

What pride is this? Who does David think he is? He's just a child compared to the seasoned Israelite soldiers and just an ant compared to Goliath. Seriously? What arrogance! What ego seemed to be on display.

But what man thinks is immaterial to God. He examines our motives, and He expects obedience. When we look again at these two kings, there is one key difference. And this difference is the distinction between pride and humility, for them and us.

Saul's focus was on the circumstances and how he could maintain control. In other words, he was comparing himself to the situation and finding himself either equal to the task or lacking. If he found himself unable to perform to public expectations, he acted out of fear. He did whatever he could humanly do to try to make things right.

David did not stop to think about what *he* could or could not do. He did not compare himself to the situation at all. Instead, David compared *God* to the problem and found his Lord more than able to handle the outcome. Maybe this is why he was called a man after God's own heart.

David didn't worry about being the youngest of eight sons, the one who was considered the runt, sent out to watch over the sheep in the wilderness. He only saw that the God of Israel is mighty. The God who empowered him to protect the sheep is also the protector of His chosen people.

So in the end, the question is simple. Who do you look to for help in any situation? A truly humble person is not one who cowers before others, always deferring and hesitant to give an opinion. In the sight of God, a humble person stands in the strength of the Lord alone, by His Word, embracing the identity He gives and not what human opinion and situational pressures demand.

How do you look at your life, your situation, and your destiny? That will be the deciding factor. To be truly humble, you will not look at yourself at all. You will only see the one who is equal to the task. We must all look like sheep to the Shepherd of our souls for all things. Pride will look to other pastures, compete with the other sheep, never be satisfied, and always feel inadequate. But we are His, and He is able to care for us. If you trust in this, you have found humility. We must not allow our attention to wander from the only One who is able to perform His will in and through us.

Another example is Esther versus the other competitors for the position as queen.

Esther's Heart

Now hear our desire,
The chosen ones say.
Our souls are afire.
We demand our way.

Give us our fill
Of blessings and good.
Bend to our will
As we think you should.

> But I require nothing
> But what he would give
> To enter his presence,
> To see him and live.

We will have blessings—
All the earthly delights
Adorned with the dressings
We see as our rights.

When we come to his chambers,
His favor to seek,
He'll find by our labors
Our station will speak.

> But I ask for nothing
> But what he requires.
> To be in his presence
> My only desire

So why are you choosing
The one who is plain?

Why are we losing
What we sought to gain?

    She required nothing
    But the king she has seen
    Bring her the crown,
    For she is my queen!

What Somebody said: Psalm 25:9; Proverbs 22:4; Philippians 2:3; James 4:6; 1 Peter 5:6

SECTION 2

NOBODY'S LISTENING:

LESSONS FOR THE ONE WITH EARS TO HEAR

4

IT JUST AIN'T NATURAL: A GARDEN LESSON

The Lord is always speaking. We just aren't usually listening. That's one reason why I believe in keeping a journal. Because on those rare occasions when we actually hear His voice and understand what He's saying to us, we should write it down before we forget entirely. When we look back at what He's told us, we are surprised by the profundity of it.

I love gardening, and more than once Holy Spirit has spoken into my life through that pursuit. My journal reflects the lessons I have learned along with my efforts to grow a diversity of crops. I enjoy preparing the earth to receive the seed. I enjoy organizing the rows and interring lifeless, dry seeds into their little graves, only to find a couple of weeks later that they've been miraculously resurrected and drawn to the light of the sun. I love the way they create their own little ecosystem for ladybugs, butterflies, birds, toads, and garter snakes.

I don't enjoy the insects and animal pests that come bent on destruction, and I try to be prepared for them so the plants can flourish to their maximum capacity. I am forever in wonder at how one seed can multiply into many meals and how quickly invading critters can deny the fruits of my labor to myself and my family.

Gardening is challenging and rewarding, a royal pain and a source of personal satisfaction. In short, it's just plain awesome.

Once, over twenty years ago, we owned a house with about six acres of hayfield. I decided to claim one corner of the field for a garden. The first year was challenging. It wasn't easy to get to the bottom of the grass and convince the earth to give us veggies for humans instead of feed for livestock.

That first year we grew as much grass as food. In our ignorance, we didn't leave enough room between rows for a tiller, so the hay that was now a natural part of the soil took over. Although I managed to dig some produce out of the nearly hip-high mess, it wasn't a pleasant experience.

After a few years of persistent tilling and natural fertilizer, the garden was finally producing wonderfully. But it continued to be a challenge to stay ahead of various types of weeds, and every year we had to harvest any larger-sized stones that worked their way up from somewhere in the depths before planting. One day, as I looked across my beautiful garden, I heard the Lord whisper, "It's not natural."

When the Lord speaks, it's not just words. It's a revelation. With those words, He showed me life from a whole new perspective. Just before Holy Spirit spoke, I had been thinking that if I didn't go out and work daily to create this space for our food, it would very quickly go back to being part of the hayfield. Within a year or two, passersby would never know there had ever been a garden there.

I saw that although the earth was perfectly capable of growing what I planted in it, it was not natural for it. It wouldn't naturally produce tomatoes, potatoes, beans, cantaloupes, or herbs unless someone put forth the effort to not only plant and water but also protect the produce from being overtaken by nature's inclinations.

Do you see the parallel to Christian life? We are all like that hayfield. Our lives produce those things that come naturally to the flesh; carnal selfishness, pride, competition, and rebellion grow so effortlessly that some believe they demonstrate strength of character.

As hay has its purposes, so all our natural attributes make a place for us in the world.

But if we wish to belong to a heavenly kingdom, we must produce an entirely different, seemingly unnatural crop. Unquenchable love by the Spirit, peace beyond understanding, joy beyond words or reason, inexplicable patience, gentleness, and self-control. Unshakable faith, uncompromising integrity, unfashionable honesty, and humility are sown into us by unseen hands, watered by supernatural springs, and fed by heavenly breath and eternal Light.

Natural? No. Miraculous? Yes, and wonderful. It's not natural. It's Christ in us, the hope of glory!

♥

A heavenly field
Sown in tears,
Reaped with joy,
Sown in righteousness,
Reaped with eternal love.
Let the seed of the Master
Reach good ground
Plowed by repentance,
Prepared by new birth,
Bountifully planted,
Abundantly gathered,
Sown of the spirit,
Incorruptible seed.
Fields white for harvest
Fruit of the King.

What Somebody said: Psalm 128:1–2; Proverbs 12:14; Isaiah 3:10; Hosea 10:12; Matthew 13; John 15:1

5

GOD DOES NOT CHANGE: A WALKING LESSON

◇◇◇◇◇◇◇◇

There is therefore now no condemnation
for those who are in Christ Jesus
—Romans 8:1

Condemnation: to say in a strong and definite way that someone or something is bad or wrong: to cause to suffer or live in difficult or unpleasant conditions; an incriminating sentence (judgment).

I know as well as anyone what it is to live with both external and internal condemnation. From early childhood, it was made clear to me that I was an unexceptional, unacceptable person. There was very little hope of future success. I often wondered why I was forced to continue living such a life. Many times I just wanted the torment to end.

Then my wonderful Savior came to me. I found hope, acceptance, and Someone who loved me in spite of me being, well, me. I devoured the Word like a starving orphan. I clung to Jesus like a barnacle, sucking in every wave of revelation about who He is, what He has done, and what He has promised.

Of course, I still didn't believe I was personally worth anything. But He loved me anyway, and that was an amazing thing. I didn't have to have value for Him to love me. He is the valuable One, the Worthy One. That's all that counts. Right?

My first marriage lasted over thirty years. We had three wonderful sons. But all marriages have their ups and downs. And I was convinced time and again that I was to blame. Again and again, I was reminded of my shortcomings—that I was not a good wife or a good mother. I was told I was incapable of love. The list of counts against me was too long to keep track of.

I was condemned. Sentenced. Doomed.

At one point, I took long, soothing walks along nearby irrigation canals. I would look across the fields and cry out to God. I felt it wasn't possible for me to be saved and be all the things I was told I was. It was too great a contradiction. And I knew a Holy God could never accept such a person. I would have to burn in hell. It seemed there was no alternative.

Even knowing Christ died on the cross did not save me from myself. In fact, it only made me more despicable that in light of His efforts to save me, I was still such a failure.

Looking back, I realize how ridiculous such thinking is and how it degrades the sacrifice He made for me. I believed in Him, but I really didn't know Him. And I didn't know myself in Him.

I only knew the sentence imposed on me by man. So I looked up, a broken and completely deceived victim of my own ignorance, and cried out, "Even if I have to burn in hell, I will still look up and praise You, Lord, because You are holy. You are good. And that will never change!"

And then I stopped, stood still, and suddenly *knew* something. *He does not change.*

A little seed sprouted in me. A seed of hope. It didn't matter what anyone else said. It didn't matter what I thought about it or what I thought about me. *He does not change.* It was one of the hardest things for me to do, but I knew I had to accept by faith that He loved me for myself, that I was qualified to enter paradise because He says so, that I can be an overcomer because *He does not change.*

♥

I am His beloved child, and no one can take me from His hand. This will always be true, because *He does not change* (John 10:27–29).

I can accept that He is guiding me and I am not a failure, because He lives in me and I am able to love because His love is alive in me, and *He does not change* (1 John 4:16, 19; 17:26).

I can be a blessing, bring light, speak peace, and have complete assurance of His call and purpose for my life because *He does not change* (Matthew 5:14, 16; Roman 8:16).

His Word applies to me today and tomorrow and the next day. His mercy extends to me every time I call out to Him. His grace paves the road I walk. His love is the air I breathe. I am Him, and He is in me because He wants it that way, and *He does not change* (Isaiah 30:18; 2 Corinthians 9:8; Matthew 24:35).

I don't have to be perfect. I just have to be His, and I become beloved, chosen, royal, and a child of destiny. There's only one reason I can be these things. I live only because He grants me life and has a purpose for my existence, and *He does not change* (1 Peter 2:4, 9–10; Psalm 100:3).

I am not alone. I am a citizen of a holy nation, a people of destiny. We will endure to the end because He has decreed it for us, and *He does not change!* (Revelation 1:5–6; Matthew 28:20).

Do you believe this? Oh, I pray you do!

6

POINTS OF VIEW:
THE TREE LESSON

Every good gift and every perfect gift is from above,
and cometh down from the Father of lights, with whom
is no variableness, neither shadow of turning.
—James 1:17 (KJV)

For the first two decades of my Christian life, I studied no Bible translation other than the King James Version. I soaked up the Word like a sponge. From beginning to end, I found life in it, but also many mysteries. The above scripture from the book of James was one of those mysteries.

The last part had me stumped. Variableness? Shadow of turning? The meaning may be obvious to some. But I was just a kid when I first read it, and it made no sense to me.

About the time I graduated from high school, my parents decided to buy a house in a different part of town. The house was on a long road with scattered houses, treed lots, and fields. In that part of the country grow live oaks, hundreds of years old, that spread their huge limbs as wide as the tree is high. With relatively small leaves, these behemoths showcase their branches like contestants in a strong-man competition.

One such tree stood proudly in the center of an empty field along the road. One day, as I drove by and admired the sight as I always did, I received a revelation. I had been pondering that mysterious verse in James again. As I drove by the tree, in my mind's eye, I could see its shadow moving and changing through the day. As I and others drove by, the shadow would appear in different places as the sun moved across the sky, giving passersby different points of view.

Different people would see the tree from different angles, with different shadows. They may form differing opinions about the tree and the field it stood in, depending on the time of day and their own vantage point, near or far. But when God looked at that tree, He saw every angle, every limb and leaf, and every shadow simultaneously. He knew everything there was to know about that tree.

God knows us the same way. He knows every cell in our body and every thought in our minds. He knows us as no one else can. Others see us from wherever they are in life. They see us in whatever season we, or they, happen to be in. They may form an opinion about who we are and are not. They may decide what they believe we are capable of. They may determine our value to them relative to our respective places in life.

I think we should always listen to opinions and bring them to God for interpretation. Remember that human opinions are generally subjective. Still, there may be something we need to see or learn. At other times opinions are just opinions and have no value compared to God's statement of fact. It is God's viewpoint that counts. His opinion can be banked on as accurate and relevant, no matter how things may appear to us or others.

Our faithful Lord, who sees us with perfect clarity from all points of view, knows precisely what we need and what would bring us the greatest joy. For this reason, all His "gifts" are good and perfect. The Greek word *good* here means useful, beneficial, pleasant, agreeable, upright, and excellent. The word *perfect* means finished, wanting nothing necessary to completeness, consummate human integrity and virtue, mature and fully grown.

He who began a good work in you will bring it to completion at the day of Jesus Christ (Philippians 1:6). Everything we receive from God is a gift. They are not random, feel-good gifts but purposeful, joyful gifts that will benefit our lives and aid us in completing our journey well. They are precious, well thought out, and planned with loving intention. He who sees us completely and perfectly offers complete and appropriate gifts.

It is still a mystery because we can never comprehend His love and provision for us. Oh, but we can enjoy His gifts and the One who gives them!

The Lord said to me,
Do you realize that I am totally aware of you?
I hear your breathing.
I know the beat of your heart.
I feel the rhythm of life moving through your veins.
I know your joys and your pain.
I know your thoughts as clearly as if you'd shouted them from the mountaintops—
　　the good and bad, pure and impure.
Yes, I know you that well.
I am continuously involved in your life, working in you to encourage you, to gently convict you,
　　to transform you completely for My glory.
I desire so much, beloved, that you would be as aware of Me as I am of you.
I desire that you would flow with the breath of My spirit, know My heart's rhythm,
　　move in the stream of My will,
　　be aware of My thoughts and desires for you.

Do you hear Me calling you?
I do not shout, but I speak as to a beloved one.
You are the desire of My heart.
Am I the desire of yours?

What Somebody said: Psalm 56:9–13; 139; Romans 8:27–28, 35–39; 2 Corinthians 4:16–18; 1 Peter 4:10

7

ONE STITCH AT A TIME: A SEWING LESSON

I like to sew, and I've been doing it for a long time. I've completely worn out a few sewing machines during more than five decades of stitching adventures. I even had a sewing business for eight years. I've sewn thousands of seams and hundreds of zippers and made dozens of alterations to prom dresses, wedding garments, and men's suits. I've made curtains, cushion covers, table skirts, and all kinds of bed coverings. And that's not counting the unusual projects.

Sewing baby quilts for grandbabies, hats and scarves for charity, and repairs for the family are typical productions and a joy to create. Occasionally, I even get to make something for me. And all these projects have one thing in common.

They're all made one stitch at a time.

I love the fascinating and always slightly mysterious way sewing machines work. They catch together threads from above and beneath in order to bring the fabric parts together into a neat, functional whole. But no matter how fast or slow I sew, it's simply not possible for these machines to manufacture more than one stitch at a time. Whether I'm using my 1906 treadle machine or any of the electric machines I've used since childhood, they are all singular in this point.

One stitch. It's like one breath, one heartbeat, one step, one blink of an eye. Think about this. This is our limitation. We are not able to function beyond one second at a time. We have no control over any other moment. And even in this moment, our hearts beat, we breathe, our eyes blink, and we are not, for the most part, exercising conscious control over any of these things. They are a mystery to us.

But there is a Power flowing to us and a Mind who knows precisely how long the seam of our life will be. There is a plan regarding our contribution to the fabric of the universe, and not one stitch or breath was intended to be wasted.

The One who designed and created us is the only One with knowledge of the final plan. We can rely on Him to place us and use us to the best advantage for ourselves and others. We just have to trust Him to know, not because He just wants to control us but because He understands the pattern of our lives and loves us for what is created in us. He has known our ultimate design from the beginning (Psalm 139:1–6, 18–18).

I see sewing as an act of creation. So here I hope you will indulge me again as I employ a bit of creative license. Here is a sewer's point of view of creation. Maybe it will help you see a tiny bit more into God's pattern and design.

Creation from a Seamstress's Point of View

In the beginning, God designed the heavens and earth.
> There were many pattern pieces, all carefully thought out but making no sense to anyone
> but the Designer.
>> God had carefully planned this unique creation as only a Master Designer can,
>> Brooding over each tuck and seam as He assembled His mysterious tour de force.

We all know no one sews in the dark. "Shine the Light over here!" He exclaimed. And Light shined exactly where He wanted it. So God rubbed His hands together in anticipation and set to work.

"This is good," He muttered as He began to stitch the first foundation pieces.

Day and night flowed in sheer elegance, just as He had thought they would. He

gave a satisfied nod and knew the first stage was complete.

Of course, this was no boring, shapeless piece of work. A definitive seam of horizon separated full, chromatic, blue smoothness above, called "sky," from layers and gathers of flowing silken and taffeta waters beneath.

These layers played and sparkled against day and night. "Oh, that is good," said God.

The second stage was complete.

God gathered the layers beneath the sky together into orderly pleats and seemingly random tucks, revealing rich shades of earth bursting with verdant texture and endless patterns, both bold and subtle.

The textures were all woven together with rainbow accents, hand-sewn throughout as

fruit, blossoms, and seedpods.

Only a Master Creator could begin to follow the complexity of line and feature.

But even though this heavenly production was already so astounding, it was

nowhere near finished.

This was only the completion of the third stage. And God was most

pleased with it. He called it pleasant, agreeable to the senses, rich and

valuable. It was beautiful, magnificent.

All these rich fabrics, textures, and embellishments were still mainly background for the more prominent layers to come.

The new layers would need to be highlighted with celestial accents.

The sky was emblazoned and embossed with sun, moon, and stars. But though
the sky was so brightly decorated, it was designed in such a way as to draw
attention to the earthy pieces, lighting or darkening them each in turn.

The sky lights helped to define and further illuminate the purpose of the
earth's design, making it a prepared canvas for the next stages.

God was greatly pleased with this fourth stage also.

Gathered into the folds and waves of blue waters beneath the sky, swimming creatures were designed, submerged in deep aquamarine fullness, flitting and diving, causing the waters to ebb and flow with life.

And flying beneath the lights of the sky, birds darted and dived like sparks of glitter and
jewels scattered on velvet.

The rich earth, with its leafy and fruitful accents, was suddenly inundated with
every kind of creature embellishment, generously and intricately woven into
earth's countless textures, bringing new dimension and purpose to every
previous stage. So ends the fifth stage.

God carefully and lovingly handcrafted one last addition to His masterpiece.

In fact, He considered this final step, the last piece, to be the purpose for creating the rest.

In secret delight, He shaped and prepared, guarding and hovering protectively

over a creation that was not intended to have the same destiny as the rest.

This part would not merely blend in. This part was, and forever would be,

the workings of His very heart. His eternal desire, an extension of His

own image imposed on an earthly background.

No other creator could have conceived, much less carried out, this

incredible, impossible design.

It was a design of beauty out of ugliness, redemption out of

corruption, eternity out of mortality—and ultimately,

it was a design of perfection.

God made man.

Stitched with loving intent. Embroidered with love and artistry. Knitted together with

supernatural destiny.

And God was pleased with His creation.

It was good.

It was complete.

God created everything without machinations. He bound heaven above and earth beneath by His Words alone, creating unbreakable bonds and invisible, eternal purposes.

To further sustain the piece, He endowed it with rest, allowing one age to tirelessly flow into another. But He offered His greatest creation repose in no other source but Himself.

"It is finished," said the Creator on a day when the final, eternal crimson stitch pierced through His own hands and feet and heart. Above and beneath were forever stitched together into one glorious, Heavenly Kingdom.

And God said, "It is Mine, and it is good."

So shall it ever be, for His glory and our joy. Amen.

What Somebody said: Genesis 1; Job 10:11–12; Psalm 100; John 1:1–5; Romans 1:20; 2 Corinthians 5:17

SECTION 3

NOBODY SAW IT:

DREAMS AND VISIONS

8

YOU'RE STUCK WITH ME NOW: PARTS 1 AND 2

One of the first ways Holy Spirit spoke to me was through dreams. I would like to share a few of these dreams or visions with you, because the lessons they teach are not exclusive. Not everyone has spiritual dreams. But the Lord is able to speak to anyone who seeks Him by means they will understand. If you think you have never heard God speak, it is not because He is silent.

As time goes on, I become more and more aware that God is always speaking. We just don't have ears to hear. I pray I will be able to hear Him better and that you will be challenged to share this same goal with me. He is speaking. Oh, that we will hear His voice more clearly!

The following dream (or vision—I've never been able to tell which) consists of two parts. The first occurred when I was about thirteen years old. The second part of the dream takes place about six years after the first, just after Navy boot camp. I had forgotten entirely about the first dream until the second dream. Then I remembered, and I will never forget again!

Part 1

I was lying on my bed one night when suddenly I saw the Lord Jesus passing by. He was walking just above me, straight across my bedroom. He was dressed in magnificent royal garments. The long train of His robe trailed behind Him, suspended over my bed. I was awestruck and filled with joy as I watched the Lord walking above me.

Then, as He passed by, I was suddenly filled with panic. He was leaving! He was walking right by and would soon be completely gone from sight. In desperation, I reached up and grabbed the train of his robe. When He felt the tug from His garment held tight in my grip, He stopped, turned, and looked down at me.

"Oh no! I cried. "You can't get away. I won't let You go. You're stuck with me now!" With a laugh, the Lord reached for me, and in a flash, I was walking by His side. He turned to look forward again, walking with a huge smile on His face. I walked beside Him, just looking and looking at the wonderful, beloved face. I just couldn't get enough of gazing at the Lord.

Then I woke up.

Part 2

I had been stationed in Orlando, Florida, for a six-week training course for my specialty rating. I had just left boot camp, and this was the first time I had ever actually lived anywhere close to on my own, with the freedom to choose my own actions, far away from home. On my first Sunday there, I went to the on-base chapel. During a rather strange service, the chaplain remarked, "Those Gideon people came here, trying to give me Bible. I told them, "We don't need those things here!"

I was stunned. I didn't return to that chapel, but I knew no one and had no vehicle so I felt very isolated. I had some trials to my faith during the next few weeks, including some that may be expected when there are over a hundred guys for every girl. I went to some flag football games with one guy for a short while, but he wasn't receptive to my witness or faith and we finally parted ways. I found the best way to repel unwanted advances from young sailors was to share the Gospel. They'd either agree or run away fast.

I generally found myself alone in the barracks on weekends, when all the other ladies would go off to party away those free hours. Finally, one week some of my roommates told me they were taking me with them the next weekend. They would not allow me to stay alone in the barracks again. I was still a quiet, shy girl. I had not learned how to stand up for myself. I was distressed at the possibility that these girls might carry me away to a place I didn't want to go.

On Friday afternoon, I went in and lay down on my bunk to pray. I fell asleep (or not), and suddenly I resumed the dream I had had years ago. It took up just where it had ended. I was looking at the Lord as we walked together. It was wonderful.

But then, in my peripheral vision, I began to see some movement. I found my curiosity was almost overpowering. I would glance to the side, trying to see what was going on over there, just out of my field of vision, then jerk my head back toward the Lord. As we walked, I began spending more and more time curiously looking away, and my feet began to unknowingly wander with my eyes.

Suddenly I felt a restraining tug on my sleeve. I turned and saw the Lord with a twinkle in His eye. He held onto my sleeve and said joyfully, "Oh no. You can't get away. I won't let you go. You're stuck with Me now!"

I was filled with such joy that He wanted me so. I was so glad to be chosen to walk with the King! We continued walking together, and my eyes did not wander again.

So I woke up. As I was still caught up in the wonder and joy of this dream, there was a knock at the barracks door. One of the girls came and said there was "some guy" asking for me. I couldn't imagine who it could be, since I knew no one.

Sure enough, there was a stranger at the door. He introduced himself, then told me he'd heard about me from the guy I'd gone to those flag football games with. He told me there was a Bible study for some of the ladies at his church on Friday nights and asked if I'd like to go. I think I scared him with my very enthusiastic response!

So for the last few weeks I was in Orlando, the Lord provided fellowship and ministry opportunities for me. I learned that the secret to living a victorious Christian life is to keep our eyes on Him alone. There is no one and nothing else worth our full attention!

Here I am, send me.
Here I am, use me.
Fill my mouth with Your Word.
Fill my heart with Your love.

Here I am, send me.
Here I am, use me.
Light Your fire in my spirit.
Let Your Light shine in my eyes.

Here I am.

What Somebody said: Psalm 31:7–8; 32:8; 18:22; Proverbs 3:5–6; Song of Solomon 1:4; Lamentations 3:21–23; John 10:27–28

9

VIOLIN DREAM

I had a very funny dream. I woke up laughing and continued laughing for much of the day. In my dream, I was sitting on a darkened stage in a huge auditorium. I was sitting in a folding chair, facing away from the audience (if there was one—I never looked). A music stand was in front of me with music spread out on it. In the shadows at the back of the stage was a grand piano. Someone sat quietly there at the piano, waiting.

I was given a tiny instrument case. Inside was a violin—a tiny violin like a toy. The violin had frets, which normal violins don't. There was a bow with the violin, also comically tiny. But I didn't laugh. Somehow I sensed that this was an important moment. I was to play a serious part—just one single note held out for one short stanza.

The problem is I don't play the violin. I've played "at" the guitar for years, but I wouldn't call myself good at it. I've never taken lessons. I learned because I sing and wanted a way to keep myself on key. Any musical friends of mine easily recognize my original songs because they generally have no more than three or four chords.

Yeah, that's just how good I am. But a violin? I always wanted to play one, but I've never even held one in my hands.

To add insult to injury, my friend "Sara," who is classically trained and plays brilliantly, came out and sat before me. She smiled hugely at me and leaned forward, obviously eagerly anticipating my debut. I wondered, *Why am I playing this? Why isn't Sara doing it? She's the violinist, not me!*

I looked at the music. I know enough about music to know what note I was supposed to play, but how to play it on the violin and how to sustain it on the tiny instrument? I studied the violin, fingering for a while, and somehow (it was a dream after all) thought I had it figured out. The pianist began to play. When the time came, I took a deep breath and dove in. The note was surprisingly clear and sweet—but that tiny bow! So short, I ran it up on the strings, making an awful, dissonant sound.

Then a conductor came out. He told me, "Just watch me and think about what you're doing. I'll show you when to start and stop. The pianist started again, and again I played. It was beautiful! I was awestruck at the strength of that one note. How did that happen?

I woke up and laughed. *What was that?* I wondered. The tiny toy instrument, the stage, Sara's Cheshire cat grin, the huge auditorium, and me playing that little toy instrument with such seriousness. It was hilarious. Throughout the day, I giggled whenever I remembered it. I asked the Lord about it. He didn't answer right away. He let me laugh through the day's activities.

In the early afternoon, I sat down for a quiet break from the day's chores. Suddenly, Holy Spirit spoke to me. "Because you were willing to take what was handed to you and do what was asked of you, even though it seemed impossible and ridiculous, you succeeded with My help."

I saw then that the pianist was the Lord Jesus, the Conductor was the Father, and Holy Spirit showed me what to play and how to play it. Then I wept because I saw how this was my whole life. Small, inadequate abilities and provisions—but oh so great a desire to be useful. Desperation to somehow succeed in being obedient, even when I don't know what I'm doing or why I'm doing it. Always trying, trying, trying, and often feeling foolish afterward. And like a failure.

That's not how the Father sees it. When we are willing to take what we are given and do as He instructs us, miracles happen. I once shared in church a message called "What Is in Your Hand?" The lesson begins with Moses alone in the wilderness (Exodus 3–4), at the burning bush. He was overwhelmed that God wanted to send him back to Egypt to deliver Israel from bondage. What if the Israelites didn't believe him? How could he possibly succeed?

God asked him what was in his hand. It was that ordinary, poor shepherd's staff that would facilitate miracles and lead God's flock to new, free pastures. All Moses had to do was throw it down, pick it up, hold it high, and God did the rest.

What is in your hand? Are you willing to use that tool, that instrument, for God's glory? Are you willing to try, even if it seems ridiculous or inadequate? Are you ready to follow the instructions that lead to extraordinary results? Simple instructions for simplistic humans, in the hand of an almighty God. That's the stuff of miracles.

The success of every effort
Is through the strength of His hand.
When we are weakest,
He is strongest.
And as He wills,
We can.

He gives power to the weak.
To the weary, He gives rest.
When He is for us,
No curse can stop us,
For through His love,
We're blessed.

What Somebody said: Matthew 11:25; Acts 4:13; 1 Corinthians 1:5–29; 2 Corinthians 4:7

10

THE GLORY VISION

~~~~~~~~~~~~~~~

I have been blessed with several visions and dreams about heaven, about both getting there and being there. The dreams the Lord has given me over the years, along with the wonderful promises in His Word, have changed my dread of physical death to longing for what comes after.

This little vision is special to me because it is a small taste of the inner sanctum, the throne room of God. As a worship leader, I would love every congregant to experience just one moment in God's throne room. Oh, how our whole idea of worship would change, and our longing for His presence would cause us to seek His face with new intensity!

At the time of this vision, I was in the midst of new experiences in "church" meetings. I had known only formulaic services, each one a cookie-cutter copy of the last. But I discovered that there are congregations that seem to flow in a different current than the stagnate waters of many traditional worship services.

It's established that I'm not a great somebody. But over the years, I have been a witness to many different moves of Holy Spirit. I have never been outside the US, but I have attended churches from California to Maryland to Florida. I have visited tiny, steepled country churches, storefront churches, denomination-steeped churches, and nondenominational churches. I believe there are reasons for them all. As Paul said, we use all means to touch all people so that by all means, we may reach some (1 Corinthians 9:22).

The glory vision took place in a charismatic church in Oakland, California. The sanctuary was packed. I don't think there was even any standing room left. The music portion of the services often lasted at least two hours, but no one noticed the time passing. We sang, we danced, and we shouted. We wept, laughed, and sometimes knelt or lay on the floor in surrender. We employed every available flavor of worship as we feasted on the glorious presence of the Lord. It was not unusual to see a "glory cloud" hovering over the front platform, but there were no special lights or effects.

On this particular Sunday night, I arrived a bit late and the worship service was fully underway. I jumped right in with the rest. I stood in the middle of the back of the sanctuary, enjoying God's presence with the other enthusiastic believers.

Suddenly, I was surrounded by an intense brightness. I was in the midst of a vast assembly of people, too many to count. We were all completely focused, with every hand reaching toward the throne of God Himself. There were colors and a moving cloud of glory all around the throne. The intensity of desire and joy from this multitude is impossible to describe. There were no distractions, no wandering thoughts. Only pure worship.

As I was reaching and exalting in His presence with the great multitude, I became aware that each person was singing a song. There were no two songs alike, but each person sang the song he or she had been expressly given. But though each sang a different song, there were no musical clashes. It was not chaotic; rather, there was an indescribable order about it. Every word and note filled a space, and every person was motivated by one goal: to adore and glorify the One who sat on the throne.

And every song was heard as if it were the only song being sung. It felt like the Lord stood before each person, glorying in their worship, loving them, and singing with them. It was overwhelmingly glorious.

I think the vision only lasted a short time, maybe only a moment. Then I was back in that earthly worship service, with my fellow believers still going strong, singing in His presence. But it was not the same. I looked around because the room was suddenly dark, and I thought someone had turned out the lights. But as my eyes adjusted, I realized it was just me. I had been to a place so bright, this man-made sanctuary was dark by comparison. I had been in a place with such a roar of adoration, such clear notes of worship, that the sounds around me seemed muted and muddled.

What a glorious place is His presence. Some years later, as a worship leader, I would tell my worship team that our goal was just to be background music to Holy Spirit's work. Our job was to be in His presence and draw as many others in with us as we could. Just a moment in His presence can accomplish more than all the pretty music, all the natural efforts we can offer. Just to be there for a moment brings healing, joy, revelation, and certainty. That's what we reach for—just to be where He is. We need to remember that.

♥

You, oh Lord, are glorious:
Glorious in holiness,
Glorious in power.
Your presence is glorious.
We exult in the weight of it.

Your deeds are glorious.
Your Name is glorious.
Your reputation is glorious.
We triumph in the honor of it.

You are glorious with radiance,
Glorious in majesty.

Your Words are glorious.
We wonder at the miracle of it.

We reach for the Glorious One.
You are Glory itself.
Our glorious Beloved, we are Yours.
And it is glorious!

What Somebody said: Psalm 26:8; 57:6; Isaiah 40:5; Habakkuk 2:14; John 1:14; Hebrews 1:2–3; Revelation 4:11

11

PIECES OF THE PUZZLE

One day as I was walking along a sidewalk in our neighborhood, I had a vision. This type of vision is very unusual for me, though I've heard of others who have them all the time. The readers may judge for themselves, but I can only accept unless Holy Spirit says otherwise.

I saw people walking all around me, on the trail and in the grass. Each of them held a puzzle piece in their hand. Many seemed confused about their own "piece of the puzzle," muttering or scratching their heads in agitation.

Some people approached others to see if their pieces fit together. It was apparent that some had tried to find where their piece fit many times and were now deeply discouraged. I did not see any pieces joined together among these people. They were all in limbo, apparently, completely unsure of where they belonged.

I noticed some pieces that looked odd to me. As I came closer, I saw that the "knob" parts of their piece had been torn off and jammed into the "holes." These people were very pleased with themselves. They proclaimed that they had it all figured out—had the whole picture and there was no more mystery for them. They called to others to come and enjoy the "revelation" they had received. They claimed to have the whole truth of life and God.

Some did come around them, but few stayed for there was no

real joining possible. Those who stayed had to disregard their own puzzle piece in favor of the apparently completed miniature puzzle created by the machinations of others.

As I was watching the various dramas unfold around these disjointed puzzle pieces, I heard Holy Spirit speak to me. He said we are each given a place to fill in God's Kingdom, though it may be unclear to us how we fit in or what our contribution may be to the whole.

We must allow God to place us as He wills. Without His help, we will never find fulfillment in the body as He intends. Only He knows what the Kingdom will be when all the parts are assembled at last to His glory.

Be assured, my dear brothers and sister, God has designed a specific place for you. You will not always feel disconnected from Him or His people. Give your whole life, your "piece of the puzzle," into His hands, and allow Him to fit you in place. Then do not fight against the place He has for you, for without your piece, others will also struggle to make their proper connections and produce the greatest possible fruit during their earthly sojourns.

We are designed to reach out into others' lives. We are also designed to receive from others. God does not intend for us to live an isolated, insulated existence. With His help, we will come together in one eternal, grand picture of His grace in us. And what a wonderful whole it will be!

Together

Shall I walk alone,
Or will you walk with me?
Together we will be twice strong,
And pleasanter the path will be.

Shall I work alone,
Or will you work with me?
So more will be the laborer's joy
Wrought not by I but *we*.

Shall I sing alone,
Or will you sing with me?
Then with a harmony sublime
Will God's glory brighter be.

Shall I weep alone,
Or will you weep with me?
There is no comfort like a friend's
To bring a grieved heart ease.

Shall I pray alone,
Or will you pray with me?
No greater force to draw God's eye
Than when two or three agree.

What Somebody said: 1 Corinthians 12:12, 14–27; Romans 12:4–5; Ephesians 2:19; 4:4–7; 1 Peter 3:8

SECTION 4

NOBODY'S THINKING:

ANSWERING THE QUESTIONS

12

ABOUT GRACE

God speaks to us all by the same Holy Spirit. His Kingdom is not divided and will never fall. He will never speak anything that contradicts His Word or His purposes in the earth. Beyond that, the methods He may use to speak to individuals may be as varied as, well, the individuals themselves. But one thing is certain, and I ask you to forgive me for repeating it: He is always speaking, whether we hear it or not.

Another way Holy Spirit speaks to me is to give me a question to answer. I have concluded that He derives great pleasure in my search for the answer. He knows that I will pray, I will study, and most of all, I will listen for whatever He desires to speak to me in His time.

One day as I was doing housework and praying, I began to consider grace. The most prevalent, easy-to-understand definition of grace is "unmerited favor." This is the definition we are brought up in the church to accept without further reflection. As I was considering what grace is and how it works, Holy Spirit said quite clearly to my spirit, "There's more to it than that."

So what is grace?

I began to delve into this wonderful word. And I found what Holy Spirit spoke was true. There's a lot more to grace than the simplistic phrase "unmerited favor." Here are some other attributes of grace:

- It's the divine influence Holy Spirit uses to turn us to Christ (Ephesians 2:8–9; Titus 2:11).
- It sustains us and aids our efforts as we live and work for our Lord. Grace keeps, strengthens, teaches, and stirs our faith and affection (Colossians 3:10, 16; 2 Corinthians 9:14; 12:9; Ephesians 3:7; 2 Timothy 2:1; Romans 12:6).
- It is the favor Christ shows us as He assists and strengthens us as we bear trouble and difficulties (1 Corinthians 15:10; 2 Corinthians 1:12).
- It is the kindness of a Master toward His servants (2 Corinthians 8:9; Ephesians 2:7).
- It is the divine influence upon the heart and the reflection of God's influence in our lives—shown by gratitude, joy, sweetness, loveliness, gracious speech, goodwill, and Christian virtue (Titus 2:11–13).
- Grace is indeed a free gift, a benefit, a pouring out of loving-kindness that motivates us to give thanks because He who has given the gift is worthy of praise (1 Corinthians 1:4; 15:57; 2 Corinthians 4:15).

Do you see the depth of His grace? There is, indeed, so much more to know about this simple word.

When the Lord asked, "What is grace?" I knew better than to try to answer it myself. Even as I studied, I waited for Him to give me the answer because I knew from experience that that is what He wants to do. The greatest, most profound, and most beneficial answers are always found with Him, and He will give those answers as we are willing to wait and listen. So one day He did answer. I don't think this answer was just for me. It greatly expands the original definition and helps us to know what we ask for when we ask for more grace.

So what is grace? I believe Holy Spirit spoke two amazing words to me.

"Enabling anointing."

Don't get me wrong. Unmerited favor is a true definition. But it's only one part, one layer of grace. By grace Holy Spirit makes us able to repent, able to receive forgiveness, and able to come to Him. By grace, we understand and accept the difference between a worldly and a godly lifestyle. By grace, we comprehend His Word and how we must be changed by it. By grace, we become more than servants; we become the very friends of Christ.

Oh, but grace is a marvelous, empowering force within us through His love and patience. It is the nature of His desires working in us, conforming us to His image with joyful abandon. Grace is free. It's ours for the taking. And we'll need it to our last breath. Thank You, Lord, for Your grace!

I am not what I ought to be.
I am not what I want to be.
I am not what I hope to be.
But still, I am not what I used to be.
And by the grace of God,
I am what I am. (—John Newton)

What Somebody said: Here are a few more scriptures speaking about the manifestation of grace: John 1:16; Acts 4:33; 6:8; 14:3; 1 Corinthians 3:10; 1 Peter 4:10.

13

ABOUT BEING THANKFUL

~~~~~~~~~~

During a difficult time in my life, when it was necessary to completely reevaluate everything I knew and start anew, I prayed for direction. Holy Spirit said to me, "There are two things you must learn above all others: how to love and how to be thankful."

I know He did not say this because I had never given or received love or because I have an ungrateful heart. Indeed, I have often been in awe of the amazing blessings I enjoy every day on so many levels. But there is much more to being thankful than just listing the stuff you have or the people you love and being glad you have them.

If you had nothing and no one, could you still be thankful? As I have read the stories of those persecuted for their faith, this attribute truly stands out. Even in horrendous circumstances, these precious brothers and sisters in Christ often return to this theme. They are thankful (Psalm 106:1). They are thankful for salvation (Colossians 1:12). They are thankful for the opportunities presented to them to share their faith (Acts 5:41). And they are thankful for the deep spiritual work done by suffering itself—the way it strips us to our core and brings us closer to the presence of our Lord.

What does it mean to truly be thankful? It means being mindful of God's favor, of the thousands of small comforts He bestows on us. It is being pleasing and agreeable because we have the privilege of life, and that's a marvelous thing. It means being liberal; because we have freely received, we will freely give. It means being beneficent because the best way to show how awesome it is when we find our Lord there in our need is to be there when another is in need.

Being truly thankful is inextricably tied to the hope of eternity (2 Corinthians 9:15). In the Bible, we are exhorted fifteen times to give thanks to the Lord for this one reason alone: "because His steadfast love endures forever" (Psalm 106:1). Without that hope of forever, it would be difficult to stand against either the tribulations or the temptations of the world. We are thankful because none of these things last forever. But His steadfast love does.

Being thankful changes our whole worldview and spiritual view. Suddenly, we see the inherent value of both the blessings and trials of our lives. Suddenly there is a light in every dark corner and hope in every rocky, narrow place. A thankful person is a friend of God. A thankful person is doing God's will (1 Thessalonians 5:18).

I read a story once of a nineteenth-century little girl who was dying, and her bed was set beneath a window so that she could look out at the ever-changing sky. She had been bedridden for some time and was often alone. She loved to be able to look out the window at the endless sky beyond. One evening a relative came to sit with her and found the sweet child in tears. When asked why she wept, she looked out the window and told her visitor that she was naming something she was thankful for as she looked at each star.

When asked again why this made her cry, she exclaimed, "Because there aren't enough stars!" I wasn't able to find this story again to verify it, but the concept of it is true. If you think you would run out of things to be thankful for long before you run out of stars, before you run out of earthly life itself, you have much to learn about being thankful.

Being thankful is a way of life. As I write this, I am thankful. I am thankful for my two eyes that see. I am thankful for my fingers that type and for the keyboard that makes it so easy. I am thankful for my comfortable home and the beloved ones who live in it. I am thankful for clothing, food, drink, and all the lovely green, living things outside my window. I'm thankful for the birds that flit by, the sounds of children on the sidewalk, electricity, the hot shower I enjoyed this morning, the soft carpet under my feet, and the adoring look of my beloved pet. Yes, I am thankful for *everything*.

And how many breaths have I taken as I was writing that paragraph? Having struggled with asthma, I can guarantee I'm thankful for every breath I am blessed to take. How many times has my heart beat without my thinking about it? How many times did the heavenly being cry, "Holy!" before the throne? Did my Lord ever take His eye from me as I wrote? Thankfully, no, never!

Do you understand? Even when I am in pain, sick, disappointed, or afraid, He is still watching over me. And oh, I am so thankful for that. My heart becomes light in His presence, and all else becomes secondary. There is always a reason to be thankful, always a hope, and always His love. Being thankful is as everlasting as our Lord. We live in eternity when we live in thankfulness. He is worthy, and we are eternally grateful (Colossians 3:15–16).

Now Thank We All Our God

Now thank we all our God
With hearts and hands and voices
Who wondrous things has done,
In whom this world rejoices;
Who from our mothers' arms
Has blessed us on our way
With countless gifts of love
And still is ours today. (Martin Rinkart, 1636)

What Somebody said: Psalm 30:4; 92:1; 100:4; Ephesians 5:18–20; Philippians 4:6; Hebrews 13:15

14

ABOUT LOVE

Both giving and receiving love have been among the greatest challenges of my life. We are often subconsciously taught to treat love like a wage to be earned rather than a gift to be given from a very young age. And the price is often higher than we are capable of paying.

As a child, I had no concept of unconditional love, and I know I am not the only child to be raised without that incredible gift. I knew I always fell short of the requirements of some elusive, favorable regard. I was convinced I was not loveable and should not expect to ever be so. So I eventually stopped trying and accepted my own unworthiness.

It has taken most of a lifetime, but I have learned one truth. Love has nothing to do with worthiness (Romans 5:8). It is not about personal qualifications. It cannot be earned, no matter how we try to manipulate the object of our affection with a display of appropriate words or gifts. The world around us, every person we know, may call that love, but it is not.

Love is both the simplest and most complex force in the universe. It is simple in that it's built into us as instinctual, emotional responses. It is complex in the motivations and definitions it inspires. How can we truly define love? How does it break us down and build us up from the most primal levels to the highest peaks of existence?

The very idea of love has become so tainted over time that it seems there should be a different word to use for what it truly is.

Maybe there is. It's a name, and He is love by definition (1 John 4:8).

From a purely human point of view, love is a wonderful, fickle, emotional, and painful thing that everyone wants and very few truly attain. This human point of view is unreliable and leads only to disappointment. Indeed, there can be no true concept of what love is apart from a right concept of God, because only God is true and truly love. All human love mimics or counterfeits that which is found in the nature of deity. So it is not surprising that, in the end, we're clueless.

Love is too powerful to control, too pure to manipulate, too self-sacrificing to be put off by the shortcomings of the beloved. Even when disappointed, true love continues to reach out and draw the beloved in, to build up and speak the truth that will make the beloved one whole and accepted. Love covers over the sins of the beloved, not with excuses or pride but with light and humility. Love reveals every corner for the purpose of occupying them with grace and joy, not controlling them with guilt and lording over them without mercy.

I feel I must make a note here. I do not mean to say that people who remove themselves from an abusive relationship do not love. These abuses must come to light for what they are. It is not love to physically, mentally, and emotionally wound another. The love the Lord has for us is full of wisdom, and the best expression of love can be prayer and honesty in opposition to fear and subservience.

True love is impossible from a human standpoint. We who are by nature selfish and biased literally have no point of reference from which to comprehend love. We live in fear of the requirement of some great sacrifice of our essential self. And so, by a great sacrifice, love has been demonstrated for our simple minds to see (1 John 4:19). A cross, an empty tomb, and the plain and simple statement: God the Father loves us so much He gave His only Son, the Son loves us so much He came to claim us for glory, and Holy Spirit loves us enough to be our Teacher and seal us for eternal life. This is beyond human faculties to grasp.

So many don't.

Love is so complex that the world could not contain an adequate explanation any more than it could hold the books containing all the words and works of Christ (John 21:25). But there is one simple word that encompasses where love begins for us.

Acceptance.

As a toddler runs into the arms of a parent and nestles there, expecting affection, protection, and comfort because it ought to be the nature and desire of the parent to give it, so we must come. It is the source of all that is needed for life and security. We must accept that He loves us. Even when we have misbehaved, even when we are glaringly imperfect, weak, and ignorant. Even when the temptation is to cover ourselves and hide from the truth of our unfaithfulness and disobedience. Even when we've been told we are not worthy.

Even then, we must run to Him and accept His love. He does love us. He will always love us. Why? Because He *is* love. He can never be anything but who He is. Love is not blind. Love sees all, knows all, and gives all. Love never fails (1 Corinthians 13). Love never changes. We must accept the truth of this. Then we can rest in Him without fear (1 John 4:18). Then we can walk through life without condemnation (Romans 8:27–28).

I accept that He loves me because He want to, He can, and He is the embodiment of love (John 3:16). He loves me. I don't understand it, but I will accept it. My heart has become lost in His vast ocean of love, my whole life wrapped up in His joyous affection. His love has taken my whole being, and I am wholly His. There is no other force that so motivates me to love in return, that reveals truth and embraces what can be when we trust Him.

I have said all this, and I have said so little. Love is inexplicable.

God is love, my love, overwhelming and inexpressible. Words cannot define Him. And words cannot define love. It is who He is, and by His love, I stand with eternal hope and promise.

Could we with ink the ocean fill
And were the skies of parchment made
Were ev'ry stalk on earth a quill
And ev'ry man a scribe by trade
To write the love of God above
Would drain the ocean dry
Nor could the scroll contain the whole
Tho' stretched from sky to sky. ("The Love of God," Frederick M. Lehman, 1917)

What Somebody said: Romans 5:8; 8:35–39; John 17:22–23, 26; 1 John 3:1

15

ABOUT THE KINGDOM

I love the prayer we call the Lord's Prayer, although I think of it not as the Lord's Prayer but ours. If you want to read the Lord's Prayer, read John 17. It is a revelatory chapter. But the universal prayer the Lord gave to His disciples is wonderful in itself or as an outline. Personally, I believe it would be a good exercise for each believer to write out, not the prayer itself but what each phrase means to them when they pray it, what thoughts come to mind, and what they are hoping for.

Some of my favorite phrases in this prayer are "Thy kingdom come, Thy will be done; on earth, as it is in heaven."

Your kingdom, Lord. Bring Your kingdom to us.

And what is His kingdom? Who are the citizens? Where is this fantastic kingdom now that the Messiah Himself would have us focus on it and pray that it would come? And what will that kingdom be like for us? How can we tell if it's coming, or has come, or our part in its coming?

Do you know that Jesus came to bring a spiritual revolution? Do you know that He came to initiate the rule of a kingdom, not a social assembly or religious hierarchy? Are you sure you really want this kingdom to come? The aphorism "Be careful what you ask for" comes to mind. Here are a few things every believer should know about the kingdom Jesus purposes to bring, and has brought already, to the earth:

- It's not "church" as many think of it. The New Testament Greek word many translate as "church," *ekklesia*, literally means "called out" and refers to a gathering of citizens called out from their homes to meet for a common purpose. It was not a word normally associated with religion in Jesus's time but rather governance. At the very least, it would have been apparent that the Lord wasn't just designating a new religious order to compete with the Jewish hierarchy of that time.

The word *church* as defined by our present religious, historical, and linguistic roots is not in the Bible at all. But some of its pagan connotation can, unfortunately, be seen reflected in the traditions of church organizations today. Christ's body is built as an eternal kingdom, not a new set of earthly rules that can be easily twisted to suit man's inclinations (Ephesians 1:22).

- It is a dictatorship. There is one King, His dictates are absolute, and He will not be changed by outside opinions. He will never be moved by political correctness, changing moral standards, or denominational adjustments to dogma (Matthew 7:21).

At the same time, this particular King loves each and every one of His subjects so intensely that He desires fellowship and friendship with them individually. The kingdom is exclusively His. He has already determined the rule of it, the size, the requirements of citizenship, and the duration of the kingdom. In this we have no say. We don't need it. Every part of the setup is for our benefit, and there will be nothing there to complain about.

For that matter, Jesus told us already where to look for the kingdom. Though it is as yet invisible to the world, His kingdom has already come. It is within us now, and we have no reason to doubt His Word or the wisdom of His reign (Luke 17:21).

• It is **Holy.** To be holy means to be separate—not integrated into the world's culture (Romans 14:17). This is a kingdom absolutely separate from earthly concerns (1 Corinthians 15:50). It cannot and will not be compromised (1 Corinthians 6:9–10). We cannot bring sin, anger, pride, or personal ambition into that kingdom. It is impossible for any earthly motive to survive there. There is no hiding place there. There are no dark corners for intrigue.

Our goal must be to bring the kingdom into the world, not the world into the kingdom.

How serious are we about God's kingdom? It is unimaginable that the Lord would instruct one of His trusted angels and they would ignore or flatly refuse to follow His commands. When we pray, "Your kingdom come, Your will be done on earth, as it is in heaven," we submit ourselves to obey as all the creatures in God's direct presence do. And why not? Holy Spirit is with us and in us, so we also dwell continually in His presence and under His rule.

We want to see the whole world submitted to Him. We want to see the kingdom of heaven come to earth. Let us not hinder His coming with doubt and disobedience.

Let Your kingdom come, Lord. Let Your will be done!

♥

This is what Holy Spirit spoke to me one day about the coming of His kingdom:

You look for My return,
    but are you really prepared for that change?
Do you have any idea how different My kingdom is from your world?
You are comfortable where you are.
You are familiar with the air you breathe, the ground beneath your feet,
    and the push and shove of the people of the earth.
You know so little of My existence in comparison.
Your world is so dark compared to My Light.
Your world is filled with anger, covetousness, and self-serving—
    so much so that you often don't even recognize these attributes
    in others you love
    or even in yourself.
In My kingdom, there is no place to hide these things.
Everything is open. All things are known.
There will be no compromises hidden away so others will see you as purer,
    holier than you are.
In My kingdom, there is no fear, no need, no desire unfulfilled.
We will be one, all My chosen ones with Me
    in understanding and purpose.
It is only at that time that you will finally know who you are,
    who I have created you to be.

You have been striving all your life to become
    what only I can make you.
But your true identity will never become reality outside of Me.
You look at that time and think of the end.
You ought to call it the beginning.
Are you ready to begin truly living?

I am fervently awaiting the Father's nod.
We are ready for the beginning of your true life.
Are you ready?
   Are you?

See 1 John 3:2 (Amplified Bible).

What Somebody said: More about the kingdom. It is the following:

- Eternal: Psalm 145:13; Daniel 4:3
- Just: Isaiah 9:7; Psalm 45:6
- Glorious: Psalm 145:12; Isaiah 11:10; Jeremiah 17:12; Matthew 25:31
- Within us: Luke 12:32; 12:21; Colossians 1:13
- Not earthly: John 18:36; Romans 14:17; 1 Corinthians 15:50

16

ABOUT REST

In the Genesis account of creation, we are told that God rested on the seventh day. Why? Was He tired? Or was He just so pleased with the results of His work He found it expedient to take off a day just to enjoy it?

The scriptures make it clear that God does not become tired (Isaiah 40:28; Psalm 121:4). He does not suffer from overexertion or burnout (Isaiah 27:3; Matthew 28:20). He is never stressed out or anxious. Yet He rested on the seventh day. If it was not beneficial for Himself, why do it?

God does not do anything without a reason. Ever. In this case, as God was creating the world, it seems that all He made was for the sustenance and pleasure of that being into whom He breathed life on the sixth day: man. As Jesus told the Jewish religious leader, the Sabbath was made for man, not man for the Sabbath (Mark 2:27).

He made rest. He made it for us. He did it so that we could take time to enjoy all that He created, just as He had Himself. He did it so that we would take time to consider as a community the power, glory, and graciousness of our God. He did it so that our body, mind, and spirit would have the opportunity to process and recover from daily stresses and activities. He did it so that we would come to Him and find the ultimate rest.

The New Testament has some revealing things to say about rest.

It seems that rest and the Sabbath are suddenly not synonymous. In fact, the Sabbath was one of the main areas of contention between Jesus and the Jewish leaders. They appeared to have no clue what that day was all about. Jesus tried again and again to turn their way of thinking from legalism to grace, mercy, and rest. They were having none of it.

Hebrews tells us that there is a rest into which we may enter by choice. It is a place in Christ that has nothing to do with any day of the week, a place constantly available to any who need it. It is a place of permanent residence entered by faith. It is the place of promise, an inheritance, like the land God promised to the descendants of Abraham. It is a place to set up house and stay in His presence, His faithfulness, and His peace (Hebrews 4:1–11).

Paul rings the death knell for the legalistic Sabbath in Romans 14:5, when he states that one person may honor one day above others, while another considers all days the same. He simply says that each person should be convinced that his own actions are right for himself before God. He makes it clear that others have no right to judge. And the Jewish-Christian leaders of the early church did not require the new Gentile converts to keep the Sabbath day. They recognized that it was not necessary for salvation.

I have always felt my ministry to be in the house of the Lord. I am not an evangelist by calling, though I believe we should always be ready to share the good news as the door opens for us. But my call is to encourage, pray, and try to speak the Lord's Word in an applicable way to God's people.

So I have been faithful to the local church. I have never been one just to attend services, sit in a pew, and be satisfied. I've worked in the nursery, taught Sunday school and children's church, performed in puppet ministry, and sung in the choir and on worship teams. I have been a worship leader and, occasionally, a speaker.

But I also went through a period of time when I didn't fit anywhere. I went to church after church for about twelve years, never finding a place where I had the peace of the Spirit to stay, dig in, and plant something to watch it grow. During that time, the Lord showed me a lot about the difference between religious dogma and rest.

I was still active in ministry during this time. I attended prayer and worship groups that met in homes on different days of the week. Somehow that Lord was still there, even though it wasn't Saturday or Sunday. I enjoyed contributing to these groups and receiving ministry from them. I felt I was where God wanted me to be at that time. His rest requires no religious rite or rule. It only requires obedience, trusting Him, and spending time in His Word and presence.

Rest is not going to church, although it's essential to join with other believers in obedience to Holy Spirit's leading. There are many who never miss a church service but are not at rest in their spirit. Rest is a place where we can live always. We can rest in Him at any time and at all times. We don't have to wait for a particular time or day. Rest is the promised land for the soul. Rest is where we find His sanctuary created for and in us. Imagine that. What an amazing God we serve!

♥

Standing on the promises
    I cannot fall
List'ning ev'ry moment
    to the Spirit's call
Resting in my Savior,
    as my all in all
Standing on the promises of God. ("Standing on the Promises," Russell Kelso Carter, 1886)

What Somebody said: Psalm 116:7; Isaiah 32:18; Matthew 11:28; Hebrews 4:11–12

SECTION 5

NOBODY REMEMBERS:

KEEPING AN EYE ON THE GOAL

17

ABOUT THE RACE

I've never run a marathon. Decades ago, before my knees started fussing like the grumpy old men, I loved to run. I would run a few miles several days a week. Running was exhilarating. It made me feel strong and weak at the same time. I felt I was capable of much more than I would otherwise have thought possible. I also felt my limitations dragging me down.

Life is like that, too. I'm sure that's why Paul used the illustration of running a race when speaking of keeping the faith to the end. He admonished the Corinthians and us also to run in such a way as to receive the prize. The Greek word Paul uses in 1 Corinthians 9:24 is *trechō,* which literally means to run a race, to be in a hurry, to spread the word quickly, to exert oneself, strive hard, and spend one's strength in performing or attaining a goal.

There is hardly an activity requiring more physical exertion of the whole body than running. Running a marathon requires strength, stamina, and mental stability. There are many moments along the way when a runner may question why they are putting forth the effort. And so we may sometimes wonder why we continue to pray, why we continue to hold to our confession of faith, why we continue to meet with the body of Christ, study the Word, and turn from enjoyable earthly pursuits in favor of obedience.

It's because the prize is worth it. Hebrews 12:1–2 tells us Jesus continued to run the race for the joy set before Him. He could see all the new brothers and sisters who would come running after Him into the Father's open arms, and He was willing to put forth the ultimate effort to win that prize.

We are also promised a prize for finishing the race. We're promised a crown of righteousness, a new name, an eternal home, and citizenship in our Lord's eternal kingship. Spiritually speaking, we simply must keep running. We must continue to put one foot in front of the other until the race is complete. We *must* keep running. There is no other option. Unless we have this mindset, we will give in to weariness, stop short of the finish line, and lose the greatest reward.

In 2 Timothy 4:7, Paul speaks of finishing the race. Some translations use the word "course" instead of "race" here. It is a different Greek word, dromos. It speaks of our life course, career, or office. I guess this is what some would call, in the vernacular, the rat race. In a very earthly sense, Paul was called by God for a specific purpose, and he put forth his maximum effort to see it through to the end. We may not see our calling as being as impactful as Paul's, but in God's sight, it is just as significant for us to finish our course as it was for Paul to finish his.

We must keep running. We must finish with the strength He gives us for the sake of winning the prize He has promised us. I have no doubt it will be worth it.

♥

Running for the Prize

I've hit the wall.
Each step is such an effort.
I might stumble, but don't fall,
Never slacken the pace.
I've come so far,

But the road is so much longer.
Yet a promise keeps compelling me
To finish the race.

The end is worth the effort.
The victory worth the fight.
Run without a question
Through the darkness to the light.
Ahead there is a vision
Coming clearer to my eyes.
I'm running for the prize.

All around,
A multitude of witnesses
Reminding me of glory
That will soon become mine.
And even now,
I feel a strength arising.
Keep the faith, no compromising.
Don't look behind.

The end is worth the effort.
The victory worth the fight.
Run without a question
Through the darkness to the light.
Ahead there is a vision
Coming clearer to my eyes.
I'm running for the prize.

What Somebody said: Isaiah 40:31; Proverbs 4:11–12; Psalm 119:32

· 18 ·

ABOUT THE COST: WHO KILLED JESUS?

Every human being shares in the weight of sin, the gulf of the separation that necessitated the sacrifice of the only begotten Son on the cross (Romans 3:23–24). But at the same time, I have known individuals who were so focused on their share in the guilt of Christ's death that they made themselves a major player in the crucifixion. It would seem that some would share the credit in personally nailing Him to the cross, as if there could be anything to glory in when considering the deplorable state of our souls before Christ.

It is true that all have sinned and fallen short of the acceptance of God. It is true also that we, left unconfronted in that sinful state, would never consider the need for redemption (Isaiah 53:6). If left to himself, man would thoroughly enjoy his self-centered, reprobate state. Only by a sovereign act of a loving God would we even be aware of the need to be reborn, redeemed, and released from overwhelming bondage.

The entire act of salvation was wholly conceived and carried out by God alone. He loved us enough to act on our behalf, even when we were unaware of the need of such action (Romans 5:6–8). He planned it before any man could even take their first step off the cliff of pride and fall into the darkness of self-indulgent rebellion (1 Peter 1:18–21).

I have thought much about this over the years. How did it happen? How could the very Son of God become a victim of a creature so limited and powerless as man? Who really killed Jesus?

The soldiers planted that piercing crown on His head, drove the nails through His hands and feet, and stood the cross up for all to see the devastating power of the Roman justice system. They had had their sport as they beat and crucified Him, mocking and dividing the spoils. The redemption of humankind was the furthest thing from their minds They were not educated in the Jewish prophecies that must necessarily be fulfilled. To them, it was just another man, another cross, another sad and sorry duty to perform without emotion or remorse.

What about Pilate? He recognized that Jesus was a guiltless man, yet he gave in to the pressure of the religious leaders and the cries of the crowd and consented to Jesus's death, absolving his guilty conscience of any uncomfortable twinges with the washing of his hands. He sealed the fate of the Christ in order to maintain the facade of power necessary for his political standing. Surely he had a choice—or did he? Was it Pilate who killed Jesus?

Of course, we all know the Jewish leaders hated and envied Him. He threatened all they held sacred to maintain their security and influence over the Jewish people. They wanted to be rid of Him, whatever it took: bribery, a riot, anything (Matthew 12:14). They had carefully planned their moves.

Did the Pharisees, the Sanhedrin, kill Jesus? They were pleased at the time to claim that victory. But could they legitimately do so?

Judas seemed to hold some affection for the Lord, yet he betrayed Him. Why? Did he believe that by doing so, he could force Jesus's hand—that when Jesus saw no other recourse, He would finally be compelled to reveal Himself as the conquering, victorious Messiah and Judas would then share in the earthly riches of His rule and reign?

But the Lord did not behave as Judas thought He would. The Messiah stood as quiet as a lamb awaiting its time before the temple altar. Why? Why does He not speak? Where are the miracles? The angels? Can it be that Judas, by his garden kiss, became responsible for the fatal blow? Did Judas kill Jesus?

There was an evil power that sought Jesus. The very eye of Satan himself never stopped seeking an opportunity to disrupt and destroy Him. This evil drove the deceived Judas, the Jewish leader, and Pilate. Did Satan kill Jesus? Would God trust a master of corruption and deception to fulfill His plan?

Oh yes, Satan was, and is, knowledgeable of who Jesus is and of God's love for all humankind. Surely he would seek any opportunity to see to it that any one of the most insignificant prophecies would go unfulfilled, thus voiding them all and making God even as himself: a liar.

Could God allow such a possibility to exist, even for a moment? Did Satan kill Jesus?

> The Lord saw it, and it displeased him that there was no justice. He saw that there was no man, and wondered that there was no one to intercede: then his own arm brought him salvation, and his righteousness upheld him. (Isaiah 59:15–16)

> It was the will of the Lord to crush him; he has put him to grief; when his soul makes an offering for guilt, he shall see his offspring; he shall prolong his days; the will of the Lord shall prosper in his hand. (Isaiah 53:10)

> For this reason the Father loves me, because I lay down my life that I may take it up again. No one takes it from me, but I lay it down of my own accord. I have authority to lay it down, and I have authority to take it up again. This charge I have received from my Father. (John 10:17–18)

Only a holy high priest (Hebrews 9:24–26), one that was clean, could offer the sin offering for all the people and take the blood into the holiest place to sprinkle it on the mercy seat before the Lord. There was never a man so holy that he could qualify to offer this man's blood upon the altar of God's own dwelling place. There was only One qualified: God Himself, the Man, the Spirit.

Christ surrendered His mortal body and sinless blood so that He could reclaim it in the end and, in so doing, claim for us that same eternal possibility.

Acceptance. Surrender. These are our calling from a God who sovereignly bought us because of love alone. How can we deny a God like that? If we do, we will find one day that we who do not have the power He did to give ourselves life have surrendered to death.

I'm so glad now we have a glorious choice.

♥

The Eternal Heart of God

Oh Lord, You know so well the limits of my heart
For You have walked where hearts of flesh are torn apart.
You took the weight of pain; You bound it to Yourself.
It was by You alone my dying heart was held.
Your body broken,
You bore my burden
Up to a Father of compassion,
Swallowed death in holy love.
I feel Your Spirit moving in me,
Feel it pulsing all around me,
Your eternal heart, oh God.

What Somebody said: Isaiah 63:5; 1 Peter 2:24; Philippians 3:20–21

19

ABOUT THE JOY

For many years, I did not believe that happiness could ever be part of my life. Since, in my ignorance, I equated joy with happiness, there was no place for joy in my life either. I knew I could enjoy moments of joy in His presence, but it seemed like an event-centered, emotional response that was never intended to last.

I was wrong.

My love for words tripped me up this time. It taught me that happiness shares the same root as happenstance, happen, and haphazard. These words all infer the need for luck or chance before the ends can be achieved. Being happy depends on one's happenstance or just the right set of circumstances. Since my personal fortunes didn't seem all that favorable, there was no reason to be happy.

Don't misunderstand me. I was not always sad. I have never been one to mope about feeling sorry for myself. I just accepted that happiness was not to be the lot for me. I learned to take each moment as it comes with neither undue grief nor bliss. In short, I lived the vast majority of my life feeling little and not being particularly alarmed by that fact.

But one day Holy Spirit spoke to me in His gentle way. He told me I was looking at the wrong circumstances. I was looking at my difficult financial circumstances, troubled relationships, and other factors of my earthly existence. "What are your true circumstances?" He asked.

I recognized for the first time the actual reality of my circumstances. I am loved beyond measure by the Creator of the universe. I am destined to be with Him for eternity. I have been bought with the blood of the only begotten Son of God. I am protected, comforted, and taught by Him. His mercies are new every morning.

So I ought to be the happiest person in the world.

But long before He spoke to me about happiness, He began to teach me about joy.

Joy has nothing to do with happiness. The Lord allowed me to spend those years wallowing in my supposed unhappiness while He taught me the truth about joy. He wanted me to understand the difference between heavenly and earthly existence. He wanted me to see that I could experience joy at any moment, no matter how unhappy I might see myself as being.

> You make known to me the path of life; in your presence there is fullness of joy; at your right hand are pleasures forevermore. (Psalm 16:11)

So far as I have been able to discover, this Hebrew word for *joy* means gladness, mirth, pleasure, and rejoicing. This is a pleasure derived from His presence and His will alone. The biblical words for *joy* speak of a response that has nothing to do with present circumstances and everything to do with where we focus our attention and our understanding of our Lord's character and power.

Joy comes from knowing that God is in control of every part of our earthly existence and will make everything right and good in His time. Joy is having absolute confidence in His Word (Romans 8:28).

"Though you have not seen him, you love him. Though you do not now see him, you believe in him and rejoice with joy that is inexpressible and filled with glory" (1 Peter 1:8). The Greek word translated as "joy" in this passage means cheerfulness, a calm delight, and gladness. There is a calmness in pure joy—an absolute, unshakable confidence that removes all stress and anxiety.

When we come into the Lord's presence, there is a stirring in our spirit and we long to draw closer. We feel the bubbling of delight, so much contentment and peace that draw us back again and again. He Himself is our joy. True joy speaks of a secret delight, a rejoicing that always lingers just below the surface of our hearts, stirring our emotions to gladness regardless of circumstances. When we speak His name or His Word, joy bubbles up and we are exhilarated and filled with the lightness of heart that true faith brings.

What does it mean to say joy is a fruit of the Spirit? What is fruit? In human life, fruit is "the effect or consequence of an action or operation" *(Merriam-Webster's Collegiate Dictionary)*. The consequence of seeking and trusting the Lord, of coming into His presence with childlike faith and understanding that He is wiser than we are and He is for us, defending and saving us, is joy.

God's joy is there in hard times, in discouraging times, and in moments of earthly grief and inner turmoil. It hardly seems possible that joy could continue to manifest in such adverse environments, but it does because it is not of this earth. If we allow it, a quiet joy can lift and sustain us regardless of outside attacks.

Joy is for us all. It is possible. It is real. It has been offered to us as a gift. That means we don't have to try to generate it in ourselves. The question is if we are willing to receive it. In fact, joy is the foundation of happiness. If it is not produced within us by His grace, we can never truly be happy.

Rejoice in the Lord always (Philippians 4:4). Always is a long time. Again I say rejoice! It is a good thing to live in joy. It is acceptable for us to do so and pleasing in His sight. No matter what else we have or don't have, we can still have joy!

♥

The Joy of the Lord Is Your Strength

Joy is a fruit that will not grow
In nature's barren soil;
All we can boast, till Christ we know,
In vanity and toil.

But where the Lord has planted grace;
And made his glories known;
There fruits of heavenly joy and peace
Are found, and there alone.

A bleeding Saviour seen by faith,
A sense of pard'ning love;
A hope that triumphs over death,
Give joys like those above.

To take a glimpse within the veil,
To know that God is mine;
Are springs of joy that never fail,
Unspeakable divine!

These are the joys which satisfy,
And sanctify the mind;
Which make the spirit mount on high,
And leave the world behind. (John Newton)

What Somebody said: Psalm 92:4; Isaiah 35:10; Jeremiah 15:16; Romans 15:13; 1 Peter 1:8; Jude 1:24–25

20

ABOUT THE WAIT

~~~~~~~~~~~~~~~~~~~

Wait for the Lord, be strong, and let your
heart take courage; wait for the Lord!
—Psalm 27:14

Nobody likes to wait. Children may seem especially impatient, but I notice many adults afflicted with this weakness. They don't seem particularly sorry about it either. They will openly tell you how much they hate to wait, admitting with pride that they are impatient and will do whatever is necessary to shorten or eliminate the chance of having to stand still or be inactive for any period of time. They selfishly demand instant gratification and cling to self-entitlement. This applies to Christians and non-Christians alike. Ask about anyone, and they will tell you *wait* is a bad word.

And yes, this is a problem.

When we think about waiting for the Lord, waiting in His presence, waiting for Him to move, we are not speaking about the same thing as waiting in a retail checkout line, in traffic, or at the DMV. Yet His children still fidget and stomp with impatience when they don't quickly receive what they've asked for or think they deserve. They cannot wait quietly for His anointing or instructions to come. They don't see the necessity or the beauty of waiting before a worthy, mighty God.

In truth, no one actually has to wait for an audience with God.

He is there the moment we turn to Him. He is always aware of us, and He knows what we need before we ever ask. We are always in His presence. But He does not manifest Himself until we have focused our attention and desire on Him alone. He holds back until we are actually listening and receptive to His words.

This is why we need to wait. This is what we are waiting for.

The Hebrew word translated as "wait" has some interesting connotations. It's not just standing around until slow, natural processes finally bring the things you have been anticipating to you or your turn finally comes to receive the attention or needed services.

Waiting in the Bible can be likened to a cat stalking a bird The cat sees its prey, and its whole attention is on it. That cat is sure it will have a tasty morsel in the end. It moves with slow, deliberate intent. Sometimes it doesn't move at all, frozen in attention, lest it misses the chance to attain its goal. Its whole attitude shows anticipation. At the right moment, it will be ready to pounce.

I know that's a rough example, but our attention and attitude must, in some ways, be like that cat's. If the cat were just lying there lazily in the sun, waiting around for its next meal to be served up, waiting for its turn to be fed, potential prey may come and go without notice. So we are in Christ.

If we are just waiting for our next spiritual meal to be served to us by a pastor, teacher, or TV ministry, we will miss many blessings, many anointings, and many opportunities to be effective in the Kingdom. We must be waiting with alertness before God, ready to pounce on and devour the Spirit's revelations and calls.

"Lead me in your truth and teach me, for you are the God of my salvation; for you I wait all the day long" (Psalm 25:5). "Wait" in Hebrew is *qavah,* which means to expect, to await; to expect Yahweh's aid, to fix one's hope on Him; to lie in wait for.

But they who wait upon the Lord shall renew their strength; they shall mount up with wings like eagles; they shall run and not be weary; they shall walk and not faint. (Isaiah 40:31)

But if we hope for what we do not see, we wait for it with

patience. (Romans 8:25)*Wait* here is a Greek word that means to expect fully.

Wake up! We are not intended to be waiting in a drowsy stupor for something overwhelming or unavoidable to shake us out of our lethargy. We are to be expecting to hear God's voice at any moment. We are to be looking for His actions on our behalf and in the world around us. We know we will see, hear, and be surprised by His revelation continuously as we wait for him.

Waiting

I'm waiting, oh Lord,
Waiting, oh Lord.
I'm waiting, oh Lord.
I know You'll answer me.

You'll give me a new song.
You'll teach me a new way.
You'll speak, Lord,
For Your words, I've come here to wait.

I'm waiting, oh Lord,
Waiting, oh Lord.
I'm waiting, oh Lord.
I know You'll answer me.

You'll open my eyes.
You'll give me grace to walk.
You'll speak, Lord,
For Your words, I've come here to wait.

What Somebody said: Psalm 38:15; Isaiah 26:8; 33:2; Lamentations 3:25; Hosea 12:6; Romans 8:25; Galatians 5:5

SECTION 6

NOBODY'S PRAYING:
WHY SHOULD WE?

21

WITHOUT CEASING

I love to pray. For me, it's sheer folly to even get out of bed in the morning without asking for my Lord's help, care, and Spirit to get me through the day. I also love to pray with fellow believers as we join together with that "two or more" authority and power.

I've noticed, however, how difficult it is to stir up enthusiasm for believers to come together just to pray. Suddenly everyone's busy, tired, or bored. Yet the Bible tells us we should pray. And not just pray, but pray without ceasing.

Seriously? Can anyone be expected to pray unceasingly, without stopping ever? What does that even mean? Maybe I'm being too literal, but if it truly means what it seems to mean, it must be possible, or it wouldn't be written there—but how?

There are just four places where the Greek word translated "without ceasing" is found, all in the writings of Paul. Three of those places refer to prayer, including 1 Thessalonians 5:17. The last refers to continual thanksgiving. And the word really does mean *without ceasing*, without interruption, and without omission.

The key to understanding what Paul is communicating is knowing what prayer is. What does it mean to pray? When many people think of prayer, they think of kneeling at an altar of some kind or at least bowing the head. They think of taking a certain formal attitude that indicates "See, I'm praying now," to both God and man. They may think of ritualized prayers, prayer books, or other controlled recitations intended to appease the great "eye in the sky."

Those may all have their place, but they are not the essence of prayer.

On the most fundamental level, prayer is communication with an unseen God. Those who are genuinely dedicated to a lifestyle of prayer will tell you that there is a two-way conversation going on. Prayer is not just throwing some words out there in the hopes that we will receive favor and be blessed for the effort. We have a passionate, compassionate God who wants to know us and speak with us, and He's gone to ultimate lengths to make that possible.

Maybe it would help to mention a few things that are not strict requirements for prayer to take place. Of course, there are times when it is necessary to give time to specific repentance, intercession, or concentrated worship. But as we strive for twenty-four/seven communion, outward demonstrations become just one layer of contact with Holy Spirit's realm.

Kneeling is wonderful, and sometimes I think we don't do it enough. But not everyone is able to kneel, and it is not strictly required for prayer to take place. A formal location or church building is not required. Nor is there one day or time of day or night that is holier than others. In fact, there is no time or place not appropriate for a believer to speak to God.

Even spoken words are not necessary for us to be in communication with the One who knows our every thought and the intent of our hearts. At any moment, or every moment, our spirit can be in communion with the Savior of our soul, our Friend.

However, I must note here that if you *never* pray out loud, you should try it. Sometimes it's just necessary to speak or even shout for all to hear, especially ourselves. It's an excellent way to drown out other unwanted, pestering voices.

So it apparently is possible to pray without ceasing. In fact, there's no reason for us not to be in continual fellowship, allowing every facet of our lives to be touched by Holy Spirit's input—not in a spooky way but receiving wisdom and discernment via our connection with the spiritual realm.

Every moment our whole body receives vital sustenance through the blood that flows to each cell. In the same way, our spiritual selves require continual sustenance through the Word and Spirit. Jesus said we must stay attached to the vine (Him) in order to bear spiritual fruit, walk in love, and receive answers to our petitions. Continual fellowship is required. This is prayer, and this is life for us as people of faith.

♥

Prayer I

Prayer the church's banquet, angel's age,
God's breath in man returning to his birth,
The soul in paraphrase, heart on pilgrimage,
The Christian plummet sounding heav'n and earth.
Engine against the Almighty, sinner's tow'r,
Reversed thunder, Christ-side-piercing spear,
The six-days world transposing in an hour,
A kind of tune, which all things hear and fear;
Softness, and peace, and joy, and love, and bliss,
Exalted manna, gladness of the best,
Heaven in ordinary, man well drest,
The milky way, the bird of Paradise,
Church-bells beyond the stars heard, the soul's blood,
The land of spices; something understood. (George Herbert, 1593–1633)

What Somebody said: Psalm 105:4; Luke 18:1; 21:36; Ephesians 6:18; 1 Timothy 2:8; James 5:16

22

BECAUSE IT'S HIS WILL

I have noticed that there are people who believe that if they pray something, it automatically becomes God's will. If they pray for a new car, then it is God's will they have one. If they pray for a promotion, it should be expected to shortly come to pass. Whatever can be vocalized becomes an instantaneous entitlement. After all, it was prayed in His name, wasn't it?

We really ought to pay better attention to the Word. We ought to know our Lord better. Maybe then we would understand that His will is not dependent on our desires, but our desires should be dependent on His will. Then we would understand that it is not our will but His that ought to be, that must be done. Most importantly, maybe we would begin to see the differences between His will and ours.

God is not Santa Claus. He is not our slave. He is not a condescending grandfather. He is not a mail-order service center or a wealthy patron bestowing gifts upon the privileged few. He is God. He is not required to grant us our every earthly wish. We are not justified in being angry or resentful if He does not. So get over it.

> And this is the confidence that we have toward him, that if we ask anything according to his will he hears us. (1 John 5:14)

Truly, truly, I say to you, whoever believes in me will also do the works that I do; and greater works than these will he do, because I am going to the Father. Whatever you ask in my name, this I will do, that the Father may be glorified in the Son. If you ask anything in my name, I will do it. (John 14:12–14)

Truly, I say to you whatever you bind on earth shall be bound in heaven, and whatever you loose on earth shall be loosed in heaven. Again I say to you, if two of you agree on earth about anything they ask, it will be done for them by my Father in heaven. (Matthew 18:18–19)

When we read about our Lord's earthly ministry, we see very clearly that He was not concerned about earthly riches or the promotion that comes from man. Indeed, quite the opposite. Note that it was to true disciples, those who had walked away from all earthly possessions and pursuits to follow Him, that He was speaking. And in those scriptures, where He talks about the disciples praying and receiving, He was not speaking about earthly purposes but heavenly ones.

He speaks about the works He did on the earth being done again by us, and even greater ones. Any of those types of works may be requested and will be granted according to His will and our faith. He speaks about binding and loosing in the spiritual realm for the purpose of building His Kingdom. He states that these requests will be heard. Anything Holy Spirit places in our spirit to pray, request, and petition in His Name will be granted. We must continue to ask for and seek for these things for the sake of His Kingdom and glory.

If we do not pray for the glory of God and His Kingdom, we pray amiss.

> You ask and do not receive, because you ask wrongly,
> to spend it on your passions. (James 4:3)

Pray for salvation, for healing, for deliverance, and He will hear. But most importantly, pray as He instructed in Matthew 6:10. "Your kingdom come, Your will be done."

His will, not mine. His Kingdom, not my material prosperity. His purposes, not my comfort. Our Lord is a good Shepherd. He is concerned for our earthly needs, and He has promised to meet them all. (See Matthew 6:31–34.) Let's trust Him for this and focus on His Kingdom business.

> Look carefully then how you walk, not as unwise
> but as wise, making the best use of the time, because
> the days are evil. Therefore do not be foolish, but
> understand what the will of the Lord is. (Ephesians
> 5:15–17)

> For all that is in the world—the desires of the flesh
> and the desires of the eyes and pride of life—is not
> from the Father but is from the world. (1 John 2:16)

Your Kingdom come, Lord. Your will be done. His will is the only will that the citizens of His Kingdom desire to see carried out because we know Him. We know His will is our ultimate good and fulfillment, and the glory is due to Him alone because He alone is worthy of it.

♥

Let Your Kingdom Come

We are waiting, Lord.
Let this prayer be heard.
Let Your kingdom come.
Let Your Will be done.
With our eyes on You,
Lord, we cry as one.
Let Your kingdom come.
Let Your will be done.
Let Your kingdom come.
Let Your will be done.

What Somebody said: Matthew 9:38; Luke 21:36; 2 Corinthians 5:20

23

BECAUSE HIS VOICE CAN BE HEARD

Psalms 19 and 29 speak eloquently of the power of the voice of God as heard through nature and the cosmos. We also know that God's voice was heard and understood as a verbal conversation in the Old Testament by Adam and Eve, Moses, Gideon, Daniel, Isaiah, and many others.

In the New Testament, Jesus makes it clear that when His disciples heard His words, they heard the Father's voice. His voice was the voice of God spoken through earthly lips. But what of us today? Should we be able to hear the voice of God? Jesus seems to think so.

> But the Holy Spirit, whom the Father will send in my name, he will teach you all things and bring to your remembrance all that I have said to you. (John 14:26; see Acts 2:39)

> And I have other sheep that are not of this fold. I must bring them also, and they will listen to my voice. So there will be one flock, one shepherd. (John 10:16)

When the Spirit of truth comes, he will guide you
into all the truth, for he will not speak on his own
authority, but whatever he hears, he will speak, and
he will declare to you the things that are to come.
(John 16:13)

Holy Spirit speaks. He is fulfilling His role as Teacher, Prophet,
Companion, and Comforter. He is speaking, and His children hear
His voice.

I have become convinced of several ideas regarding the voice
of God over the years, and I have found no scripture to contradict
these ideas. But as I heard one southern preacher say, "Eat the corn
and throw away the cob."

1. **God's words are eternal (Psalm 119:89; Isaiah 40:8).**
    Of course they are. But to be more specific, when God
    speaks, His words go forth with purpose and continue in
    that purpose until He decides otherwise (Isaiah 55:11). For
    instance, when God said, "Let there be light," light came
    into being and has continued to shine because His words
    continue to speak and sustain that light (1 Peter 1:25). God's
    words are not like our words. So often when we speak, our
    words mean and accomplish nothing. They will not be
    long remembered, even by us. But God's words are living.
    They continue to support the existence of the world and
    everything in it (Matthew 4:4). They still speak (Matthew
    24:35).

2. **God is always speaking.** Is it really so hard to believe,
    with so many creatures in heaven and so many seeking,
    praying souls on earth, that God must, of necessity, never
    cease to speak? The only indicator of God ever being silent
    is the scripture in Revelation 8:1, when there is a half hour
    of silence in heaven. The purpose of that half hour is not
    currently known, but I've no doubt it is profound. At

present, however, we are, it seems, swimming in a spiritual sea of God's words. In fact, the entire universe is sustained by His words (Hebrews 1:3). How is it we do not hear?

3. **We could hear much more than we do now.** I often find myself not, pausing at odd moments through the day and praying, "Lord, tell me something." I long to hear His voice. His words are the most precious gift, and to know His mind is to know peace in a turbulent world. His words, both written and spoken, keep us on the right path and show us the next steps. His words are so convicting, so pure, that they can shut off our own, and that is a good thing. We so often have no concept of the folly issuing from our own mouths.

Lord, what are You saying? Tell me something. Help me to hear Your voice, to understand the life of Your Spirit pulsing around me. Lord, let me hear Your voice so that I can walk on the earth, speaking only as the Father teaches me (John 8:28).

♥

The Lord said,

I have never stopped speaking.
Every Word I have ever spoken lives eternally.
My words hover over the earth.
They continue to speak life to the earth
    as they have from the first day of creation.
If they did not,
The enemy would have brought all creation to ruin long ago.
But he cannot break through My words.
How do you not hear Me speaking?
You walk continually through an ocean of My words,
    but you do not hear.

Instead, you say, "I am so thirsty,
I will go and drink from the fountain my eyes see.
    What man provides that is treated with false hopes
    and dispensed through polluted earthly doctrine."
You drink these waters, and you are never satisfied.

Come to Me.
I still cry out to all who thirst.
Come to Me and drink the living waters.
Be satiated in My words,
    then let them flow from your inmost being—
    a cleansing, healing stream.

My words live.
None return void.
My words are in your heart, in your spirit,
    and in your mouth.
Speak My name.
Speak My promise.
Speak My power.

I have never stopped speaking,
    and neither should you.
You will hear My words and understand them
    when you speak them.

What Somebody said: John 10:27; Hebrews 12:25–29; Revelation 3:20

24

BECAUSE IT'S REAL

I read about a philosopher named Socrates. I decided, because I don't necessarily agree with everything the guy is reported to have said, or with the ridiculous notions of his greatness some people seem to hold, that there was never any such person. He's just a made-up persona, someone's attempt to bend the thinking of humanity in a chosen direction.

If Socrates did exist, he had some pretty hard notions of right and wrong. Why should I accept them? I'm perfectly capable of deciding what's right and wrong for myself. I don't need the help of kooky philosophers and their extinct groupies. I'm telling you he's not real! Nobody I know ever met the guy. All we have are centuries-old scribbles and a lot of emotional jargon, right?

If the above sounds unreal, it's because it is. Few debate that Socrates was a fifth-century BCE Greek philosopher whose writings became the fundamentals of Western thinking. Somehow, after over twenty-five centuries, he is still revered for his ideas regarding man's pursuit of happiness.

But the reality of the Living God is contested at every turn. Why is that? Can it be because knowing Him means acknowledging the darkness in ourselves and either repenting and submitting or rebelling and falling into even greater darkness?

Is God real? (Drumroll, please.)

Unequivocally YES! How do I know that? I can tell you it is not only because of the writings of the Bible, although they are indispensable. (See Romans 1:19–20.) There are those who have very little access to the written Word, yet they still believe. Why? How can they know God is real? How can anybody know?

We cannot doubt the existence of One we have met, known His presence, heard His voice, and seen His unique activities on the earth. The only authentic way to "know" the existence of anyone is by personal contact (1 John 1:1–3). Everyone else is just a story. No matter how much impersonal evidence we may have of their existence, this is undeniable material evidence. Personal contact, conversation, and relationship are the things that make a person real to us (Jeremiah 31:33–34).

But God does not flaunt Himself before humanity with overpowering supernatural events. He waits to be sought out, and then He also seeks out those whose hearts are His to own (Psalm 27:8). From the moment we meet Jesus, an eternal love affair unfolds, and the essence of our communication with Him is a process called prayer.

Why pray? Because He loves us, we love Him, we recognize His promises and power, and we need Him to sustain and fulfill our lives. The power of prayer is real because He is real. If you believe in Him, you will be moved to pray and seek Him to learn more about Him.

Let Me Live in Your House

Show me who I am.
Show me who You are.
Take me from this earthly dwelling,
Out among the stars,
And let me live.
Let me live in Your house.

Show me what is real.
Teach me how to love.
Feed me living water
And manna from above,
And let me live.
Let me live in Your house.

I want to see Your face.
I want to touch Your heart
Here in this secret place,
Where we come apart.

Show me who I am.
Show me who You are.
Take me from the earthly dwelling
To soar among the stars
And let me live.
Let me live in Your house.

What Somebody said: Psalm 84; 27:4; Isaiah 55:6; Jeremiah 29:13; Matthew 7:7; Hebrews 11:6

SECTION 7

NOBODY WAS THERE:
THE ETERNAL NOW

25

SOMETHING TO LOOK FORWARD TO

I'd like to share another interesting peek into heaven. I hope sharing my dreams does not make you uncomfortable. I see them as special gifts that make me antsy to be with my Lord in the glory to come. So I will be all the more careful about how I live on earth.

Before Jesus introduced Himself to me, I was a slave to many fears. I was afraid of the dark, crowds, heights, shadows, bugs, snakes, large animals (and some small ones), loud noises, and being alone. I was absolutely unable to speak before people. I was terrified of rejection, authority figures, and things that go bump in the night. I was, in short, one hot mess.

After my first meeting with Jesus, I was miraculously delivered from the vast majority of those fears. I was eleven years old, and my mom had started taking us four siblings to church. I was so closed off from other people I didn't remember anything about the services until after my Jesus encounter. The Sunday after meeting Jesus, which happened when I was alone in my room in the middle of the night, I turned to the girl sitting next to me in Sunday school and said hello.

The girl nearly fell off her chair. She became my first real friend, and she told me later that she'd been talking to me for weeks and

I had never responded at all. I don't recall her ever speaking to me before that fateful Sunday. That's where I was in my head, and that's where Jesus brought me from in an instant.

However, there was still one fear that kept its talons sunk deep in my soul. Death. Death was scary. Death hung around like a bully, waiting to snag another victim. Death followed me everywhere, threatening, sneering, and mocking.

So God gave a heavenly dream about what it's like to die and be personally escorted by an angel into glory. I have not been afraid of death since. It's just another door to walk through in God's time, from life on earth to life in heaven.

That dream is too long to share here. The dream I do want to share was given years after the first one and is a glimpse of what we may find in heaven itself. I know it was only a dream, but it has stuck with me and given me hope.

I was standing in a beautiful room. It was everything I love in space, color, and design. To recline on the overstuffed furniture would be like floating on a cloud. Everything was suffused with light—clean, and airy. There was a huge fireplace with a marble mantelpiece and carved wooden tables along the walls. I remember thinking how perfect it was.

On the mantel and other furniture were knickknacks. As I wondered about and began to examine some of the items more closely, I found they all reminded me of some moment or some event in my life.

I heard a voice I felt was the Lord speaking to me, though I didn't see Him there. He told me that He had placed these mementos as reminders of successfully navigating difficult times together. They were His gifts to me because He was pleased when I was obedient, faithful, and trusting.

I noticed a set of French doors in one wall of the room. When I walked through, I found myself in a magnificent, cathedrallike room. The ceilings were at least twenty feet above me, and there were many Roman-style, carved columns reflected in the polished marble floors. I wondered what the room was. I heard the Lord say, "This is where you'll dance for Me."

At this point, I woke up. I was astounded by the first room. The warmth, light, and beauty of it just seemed so perfect to me. I was even more stunned by the second room since, at least in my own opinion, I don't dance. I can't imagine even trying such a thing in front of anyone else. I have sometimes been exuberant when worshipping alone, but only the Lord could say if my movements could be defined as dance.

However, I love to watch dance and have always secretly wished I could move and embody music as dancers do. Maybe when I am in that heavenly place I will finally dance without self-consciousness for the enjoyment and glory of my Lord alone.

Jesus told His disciples that He was going to prepare heaven for them (John 14:1–3). Maybe this dream was a glimpse of my own special place. He knows each of His own so well and has planned for each a unique space that will be theirs for eternity. He watches over us to see how we will walk through every season and trial of life. He never forgets a single battle or triumph. And He loves to display His pleasure in us.

What will your room look like? I don't know, but I believe it will be perfect for you! And the reason for the perfection is that our awesome Lord will be there with us, rejoicing in our victory for eternity to come!

♥

The Spirit and the Bride Say Come

I was just a child when I first met Him,
And I knew that I would always love Him.
Now the time has come and gone.
I see how I have grown
And learned so many lessons preparing me for my new home,

How my heart is yearning.
The watching and waiting will soon be done,
The Spirit and the bride say

Come, for I am ready, clothed in spotless white
Garments washed in precious blood,
Clean now in His sight.
And now, my eyes shall see the Bridegroom,
God's own Son.
The Spirit and the bride say come.

No more strife among us, standing hand in hand
Cleansed from all iniquity, a brand-new man
Loosed from every bondage now that would have held us down.
We have held back nothing that could keep us from our crown.
Now our eyes turn upward,
And as one voice the cry's begun.
The Spirit and the bride say

Come for we are ready, clothed in spotless white,
Garments washed in precious blood
Clean now in His sight.
And now, our eyes shall see the Bridegroom,
God's own Son.
The Spirit and the bride say come!

What Somebody said: John 17:24; Colossians 1:4–5; Titus 1:2–3;
Hebrews 10:23

26

THE ETERNAL NOW

⌢⌣⌢⌣⌢⌣⌢⌣⌢⌣

I have noticed how difficult it is for some believers to let go of anger, resentment, and offense. I have watched as those who claim salvation through Christ seek to label themselves as grieved beyond comfort, wounded beyond healing, or damaged beyond repair.

How easily we put on the rags of earthly woes and parade ourselves as mental, emotional, or provisional beggars. It's so easy to glory in our infirmities, not as Paul did—to the end that God's power brings us victory in spite of them—but for the sake of our own misery. We would like to receive more pity, indulgence, emotional "support," and the time and efforts of our fellow earthlings just to prove our sad state is worth clinging to.

I would not wish to downplay the reality of suffering. Indeed, the Bible is clear that we are to pray for one another, grieve with the grieving, rejoice with the blessed, and build one another up (Romans 12:15; 1 Thessalonians 5:11). I do not condemn the physically infirm or disabled or those who grieve loved ones who have passed beyond our touch. But even in these things, I've seen eventual victory for those who will grasp it.

I have learned that the spirit is indeed able, with God's help, to overcome all things and live in His peace and comfort (2 Corinthians 1:3–4). But some apparently decide they will never be well. No matter how much we pray, some hearts do not recover, and some hands will hang down forever if others do not continually hold them up (Hebrews 12:12–13).

Maybe there are reasons for this sometimes, but I admit I find it difficult to understand. And I feel some readers need to hear the following message.

We so often live our lives looking backward. It is good to learn from the past, but we must realize that it cannot and will not change. God does not change the past. Once a moment has gone by, it is done. We can only allow God to redeem our future moments to bring Him glory.

We forget that we are eternal creatures, not just after the separation of spirit and body but now (1 Timothy 6:12; John 17:3). At this moment, we are eternal, as we will be in the next moment and next—up to the moment of the death of the flesh, when we will still proceed to the next moment, only without earthly weights to hinder us. Our moments are eternal now and forever.

So why can we not live in the glory of that eternity in this moment as we will then? Why do we hold back when we have the promise now (2 Thessalonians 2:16–17)? What keeps us from grasping the truth, the life offered by resurrection power? Why can we not see the eternal through the viscous fog of insubstantial, illusory physical being?

Maybe for some, the issue is they simply don't understand the promise of the present, but only the difficulties. Maybe some have never been taught the Word of truth or sought the answers for themselves or heard the voice of the Spirit seeking to comfort, convict, and convince them.

For others, it can only be called an act of willfulness. There are those who believe they are owed their misery, that they have been mistreated and maligned, apparently beyond what the blood of Christ, the power of His name, and the promise of the future can possibly offer. That is a perilous place to be.

God has contended for the eternal placement of every soul. He has given us who come to Him access to the heavenly throne. He has placed at our fingertips His own divine presence and wisdom. He has given us a Comforter and Guide. And He has assured us that He is with us and knows exactly where we are and what we need.

We are in eternity now. So far as God is concerned, it has already been purchased and granted to us. Let us live in the glory of it, the rest provided by it, the Eternal Presence possessing it. It is not impossible. But it is not easy. It requires that we let go of, voluntarily put off, all the self-appointed distress the world requires in order for us to appear to be normal human beings (Colossians 3:2–4).

We must accept that we are not normal human beings. We are supernaturally reborn beings in a frail human container. Still, the clay cannot contain the possibilities, or the realities, of this moment if we do not allow it to. We are, by the declaration of God, more attached to eternity than we are to limited flesh and bone. We must learn what this means. We must live in it if we truly desire to display the heavenly realm before men.

We live in eternity now, this moment. We just have to remember and act like it (2 Corinthians 4:7–18).

Time is running out.
This is the moment—
The only moment I have.
I must hear.
I must obey now, before the moment is beyond reach,
Beyond recovering.
How many moments have been lost already?
Thousands. Millions.
But this one can be glorious
If I listen. If I obey.
I will see what my eyes strain to see.
I will have what my heart longs for.
Your glory. Your presence.

Your pleasure in my small victory.
The hope You have for me,
What I will be with You,
What I am with You—
This moment,
Before it's gone,
Show me Your heart.
There're no counting moments
Beyond that one.
That moment is eternity.

What Somebody said: Ecclesiastes 3:11; John 3:16; 6:40; 10:28; Hebrews 5:8–9; 1 John 1:2; 5:10

MY THANKS

I am unspeakably thankful to all the people in my life who continue to support and believe in me, even when I don't believe in myself. Thank you to my wonderful husband, Mike, who always has my back and is usually pushing me gently along. Thanks to Pastor Dennis and Mary Ellen Schoonover, who laud me to the point of embarrassment. Maybe it helps. Thanks to my sons, Jonathan, Ben, and Ian, who think I'm fantastic. I find that humbling and motivating to excellence. Thanks to all my church family, who continually hold me up with encouragement and prayer. That's the only reason anything good happens.

The greatest thanks always goes to my faithful Lord, without whose presence nothing is worth doing, and nothing would come of what's been done. I will love Him forever.

M. A. Slatton

Printed in the United States
by Baker & Taylor Publisher Services